SHIPPING INDUSTRY IN INDIA
Colonialism to Globalisation
(*A Spatio-Temporal Analysis*)

SHIPPING INDUSTRY IN INDIA
Colonialism to Globalisation
(*A Spatio-Temporal Analysis*)

Sadanand Gupta

PENTAGON PRESS

SHIPPING INDUSTRY IN INDIA: Colonialism to Globalisation
(*A Spatio-Temporal Analysis*)
Sadanand Gupta

ISBN 978-81-8274-891-0

First Published in 2016

Published by
PENTAGON PRESS
206, Peacock Lane, Shahpur Jat,
New Delhi-110049
Phones: 011-64706243, 26491568
Telefax: 011-26490600
email: rajan@pentagonpress.in
website: www.pentagonpress.in

Branch
Flat No.213, Athena-2,
Clover Acropolis,
Viman Nagar,
Pune-411014
Email: pentagonpresspune@gmail.com

Printed at Aegean Offset Printers, Greater Noida

Dedicated to

MY BROTHER

(SRI DEVANAND GUPTA)

Contents

Acknowledgements

I would like to express my gratitude to all those people who have helped me in this endeavour. I would like to convey my thanks to the Ministry of Shipping and Indian Ports Association (IPA) for providing the data sources and library facilities.

I am much indebted to, and have a great sense of respect for, my esteemed PhD supervisor Prof. Atiya Habeeb Kidwai for her unstinted support, diligent efforts, healthy criticism, encouragement and constructive suggestions without which this work would never have evolved.

I have a deep regard for Sri Dharmendra Kumar (Director, Patanjali Institute) and Dr Alok Kumar Srivastava for his unvarying support and logical outlook.

Special thanks are also due to Mr Amit Dagar, Mr Umesh Chauhan, Mr Santosh Kumar, Mr Mohit Choudhary and Mr Praveen Bhargava for aiding me—much beyond my imagination—in the writing of this book.

I have deep regard for all my family members, especially my respected parents and my elder brother Sri Devanand Gupta, who has been instrumental to all my success and has supported me whenever I considered necessary. My thanks to my sisters, brother-in-law and sister-in-law—they all have an uncomplaining reliance on me. Without their blessings, love, emotional and moral support, this book would not have taken its present shape. The memories of the sweet and innocent smiles of my nieces and nephews also stimulated and refreshed me from time to time throughout this work.

On her part, Apoorva (my wife) has had to compromise with the time which I spent in this venture. My daughter Ananya and my son Shivansh have always invigorated me whenever I felt bored and tired. Their innocent activities and untimely interruption in the work made me pause from the work and think differently.

Special thanks to Mr Rajan Arya for his consistent endurance in accomplishing this monograph on time. I express my heartfelt gratitude to him for his loving and caring attitude and stable support especially throughout my periods of stress and strain which have always boosted my morale and confidence. He has always motivated me to do something extraordinary and has always shown firm belief in me.

Last but most importantly, the editor of the book, who has done exceptionally well in organising this book in its present shape.

A very huge thanks to you for all your love and support.

All criticism and suggestions are welcome.

Sadanand Gupta

Preface

This book has emerged out of my consistent and regular engagement with the shipping industry over the past several years. This book emanated and was chiselled from my MPhil dissertation ("Restructuring of the Major Ports of India in the Post-Reform Era") and from the honorary contribution to an ICSSR project of Prof. Atiya Habeeb Kidwai entitled "Ports as Infrastructure, Ports as Cities: The Indian Port System". The thought of publishing my research work as a book occurred at the culminating stage of my ongoing research work. I realised that there is no work on the industry which presents an integrated and balanced account incorporating other than an economic outlook in the analysis.

Having a long history of maritime trade, India has a coastline dotted with ports and port-cities, major and minor. Such an analysis involves many conceptual and theoretical issues. The discussion on the historical evolution of the seaport system of India which follows, forms the backdrop to the analysis of the growth patterns, hierarchical arrangements and the hinterlands and forelands of the Indian ports during the following periods: the colonial period, when the introverted economy of the country was reoriented and focused onto the seaports and the post-reform period when India got increasingly drawn into the world economy. The volume as well as the commodity combination of the maritime trade of India is also analysed for each of these periods. Ports are then ranked in terms of their performance and productivity. Since many Indian ports are also important cities, these port-cities are placed within the national system of ports and cities and the linkages between the port and city functions are outlined.

The policy implications of the analyses forms a substantial part of the penultimate discussion which focuses on the physical and economic factors that are of concern in port planning, as well as on the issues related to port modernisation and restructuring, management and governance.

The complexity and variety of seaport structures and functions and their socio-economic interlinkages with their hinterlands and forelands have resulted in the development of several theoretical and conceptual frameworks and analytical methodologies. Most of the existing studies on the Indian ports do not interface with these theoretical and conceptual issues necessary for a complete understanding of the port system. Ports respond differently in the periods of growth and recession. It is, therefore, necessary that a historical in-depth analysis of ports, which includes the issues of efficiency and performance, as well as management and development, is available to the port planners so that they may understand the varied responses of the ports to the cyclical nature of world trade and to the physical constraints which may at times overwhelm them. The existing historical studies are often only a ritualistic "looking back" account of the Indian ports.

Except the Introduction, this book is divided into five chapters. The Introduction deals with an overall scenario of the industry, the spatial arrangement, significance of the ports in the national and regional economy and the objectives and methodological aspects of the proceeding work. Chapter One presents a detailed account on cargo traffic, composition and volume, key geographical determinants and their impact on the overall traffic handling, identification of some of the regional-level issues in port development, etc. An all-India scenario of the shipping industry since the pre-Independence era to the post-reform era has been compared and contrasted. Chapter Two focuses on the concepts, criteria and techniques of port performance and productivity. Also in order to find the relationship between port performance, the demands of globalisation/liberalisation and the impact of corporatisation and privatisation on the functioning of the port system, a model for ranking all the major ports has been developed for comparing, computing and understanding the changing position of the ports after the post-reform era on the basis of the operational performance indicators. Chapter Three focuses on port restructuring and modernisation in the post-reform era. Ports are not isolated entities connecting to virtual value chains. They are part of a regional economy and the evolution of the regional economy strongly affects the performance of the port. It is, therefore, important that the multifaceted structure of the port system in India is analysed and the influence that these ports have on the regional development of their hinterlands gets systematically assessed. This issue forms the main concern of this chapter.

Chapter Four concentrates on the containerisation of the ports and the issues and implications of unitising the cargo for transportation, supply chain and storage. Container logistics incorporate supply, transportation, packaging, storage and security together with the visibility of the container and its contents into a distribution system from the source to the user. Chapter Five investigates the issue of governance in the port system. Currently, the Port Sector is governed by a plethora of complex laws and regulations. The Port Sector lacks an independent, full-fledged regulatory authority. At present, regulation is done through the Tariff Authority of Major Ports (TAMP), which was formed in March 1997. The Sector experiences a lack of policy measures for enhancing the production function system. A detailed analysis of the regulations and probable strategy have been proposed in the chapter for a further policy formulation.

I think that this book, being a systematic account as it is, would be useful for the government in terms of planning, for regional planners, academicians working on industrial economics, ship manufacturing firms, researchers, journalists, shipping societies, ministries, corporate bodies, etc.

All criticism and suggestions are welcome.

Sadanand Gupta

Abbreviations

BOOT	Build, Own, Operate and Transfer
BOT	Build, Operate and Transfer
CFS	Container Freight Station.
ChPT	Chennai Port Trust
CONCOR	Container Corporation of India
CoPT	Cochin Port Trust
DCI	Dredging Corporation of India
DLB	Dock Labour Board
DWT	Dead Weight Tonnage
FDI	Foreign Direct Investment
FIs	Financial Institutions
FRM	Fertiliser Raw Material
GAPL	Gujarat Adani Ports Ltd
GOI	Government of India
GPPL	Gujarat Pipavav Port Ltd
GRT	Gross Registered Tonnage
HDC	Haldia Dock Complex
ICD	Inland Container Depot
ICICI	Industrial Credit and Investment Corporation of India
IDBI	Industrial Development Bank of India

IDFC	Infrastructure Development Finance Company
IFCI	Industrial Finance Corporation of India Ltd
IIPM	Indian Institute of Port Management
IPA	Indian Port Association
JNPT	Jawaharlal Nehru Port Trust
KDS	Kolkata Dock System
KoPT	Kolkata Port Trust
KPT	Kandla Port Trust
MbPT	Mumbai Port Trust
MoPT	Mormugao Port Trust
MOST	Ministry of Surface and Transport
MPTA	Major Port Trust Act
MT	Million Tonnes
MTPA	Million Tonnes per Annum
NFTP	National Foreign Trade Policy
NIPM	National Institute of Port Management
NMPT	New Mangalore Port Trust
NSICT	Nhava Sheva International Container Terminal
POL	Petroleum, Oil & Lubricant
PPT	Paradip Port Trust
R&D	Research and Development
SPV	Special Purpose Vehicles
TAMP	Tariff Authority of Major Ports
TEU	Twenty Feet Equivalent Unit
TPT	Tuticorin Port Trust
VPT	Visakhapatnam Port Trust

List of Tables

List of Figures/Maps

Introduction

"A port is essentially an economic concept, an economic infrastructure that serves coastal and overseas traffic. Port is a sub-system of the total transport network and a meeting place of other modes of transport. A port is a gateway for the entrance from surface water to land and vice versa. Port is also constructed as the major crossroad of traffic in ideas, peoples and goods over the centuries".[1]

India is endowed with an extensive coastline of about 6,100 kms along nine coastal states—namely Gujarat, Maharashtra, Goa, Karnataka and Kerala (on the west coast) and Tamil Nadu, Andhra Pradesh, Orissa and West Bengal (on the east coast). India had only five major ports at Kolkata, Mumbai, Chennai, Cochin (Kochi) and Visakhapatanam when it became independent in 1947.[2] Today, these nine states have in all 12 major and more than 200 minor ports. Among these 12 major ports, six are located on the west coast (Kandla, Mumbai, Jawaharlal Nehru Port, Mormugao, New Mangalore and Cochin) and six on the east coast (Tuticorin, Chennai, Ennore, Paradip, Visakhapatanam and Kolkata). Four of the major ports viz, Kolkata, Mumbai, Chennai and Mormugao are more than 100 years old. The ports of Kandla, Tuticorin, New Mangalore, Haldia and Paradip came into existence after independence. The JNPT became operational after 1989. Ennore is the first major corporate port of India which started its operation in 2001.

It is worthwhile to mention here that nearly 190 years after Johann Von Thunen's *Isolated State* (1826), 86 years after Alfred Weber's theory of location of industries (1929), 60 years after August Losch's *The Economics of Location* (1954) and Walter Isward's *Location and the Space Economy* (1956) were published, nowhere in the world do spatial factors like transportation and more specifically sea transportation in regional economic development got a proper place in the textbooks.[3]

The major ports are under the purview of the Central Government, while the other ports (minor and intermediate ports) come under the jurisdiction of the respective State Governments.[4] States which have Maritime Boards are Gujarat, Maharashtra and Tamil Nadu while States without Maritime Boards are Kerala, Andhra Pradesh, Goa, Karnataka, Orissa, West Bengal and Union Territories.[5] Currently, the port sector is governed by a plethora of complex laws and regulations. These include the Indian Ports Act (1908), the Inland Vessels Act (1838), the Dock Workers (Regulation of Employment) Act (1948), the Merchant Shipping Act (1958), the Major Port Trusts Act (1963) and the Dock Workers (Safety, Health and Welfare) Act (1986).[6] The port sector lacks an independent, full-fledged regulatory authority. At present the regulation is done through the TAMP, which was formed in March 1997. Ennore is an exception here because it does not come under its jurisdiction.[7] Its functions are threefold—namely, the regulation of tariffs levied by the major port trusts and the private terminals therein, fixing rates for the services rendered as well as for the use of properties and setting the governing conditions that influence the application of rates. Overall, TAMP aims to use tariffs to bring about operational efficiency, to rationalise tariffs and to sysematise tariff-setting systems across all the major ports. But the financial institutions want these things consolidated into a single law for ensuring better performance and efficiency.[8]

The seaport and dry port systems in India are being restructured in response to the structural adjustment reforms adopted in 1991 which aimed at liberalisation/globalisation/privatisation of the country's economy. The catalysts have been three national level infrastructure and regional development programmes linked to post-reform growth strategies. These programmes involve the construction of national highways to connect the four corners of the country, making a garland of new seaports on the triangular peninsular coasts and the creation of corridors for industrial development and efficient freight movement. These programmes have created a non-path dependent trajectory in India's port sector wherein the old ports are losing their significance and a new locational matrix of sea and dry ports is being created, linked to the seaport-oriented transport/freight corridors.[9]

Ports handle 90 per cent of India's foreign trade in terms of volume and 70 per cent in terms of value. The capacity of the Indian Ports increased from 20 million tonnes (MT) of cargo handling in 1951 to 744.91 MT as on 31 March 2013.[10] Consequently, capacity is no longer a constraint for the major ports. As a result, there has been a substantial improvement in their efficiency as borne out by the reduction in waiting time for the ships. Important commodities, handled by quantity though the major ports are crude oil and petroleum products, ore (primarily iron ore), coal, fertilisers and fertiliser raw materials, foodgrains and general cargo including containers. The traffic handled by the major ports pertains to liquid cargo followed by dry cargo and the remaining general cargo.

The Statement of the Problem

The purpose of this study is to highlight the role the port plays in India's regional economic development and also to find the relationship between port performance, the demands of globlisation/liberalisation and the impact of corporatisation and privatisation. The importance of such work has increased since the initiation of the globalisation programme in 1991. No such research work exists which fully incorporates the impact of recent changes after globalisation on the port system in India.

Aims and Objectives of the Study

The following aims and objectives have been enumerated for the present study:

1. To trace the long-term trends of cargo traffic handled by the major ports, the qualitative and quantitative changes in the nature of cargo, changes in the export and import structure and container traffic at the ports.

2. To trace the evolution of the Indian seaport system from the colonial period, when the introverted economy of the country was reoriented and focused onto seaports, to the present day, when India is being increasingly drawn into the world economy.
3. To underpin the various factors which have historically influenced the performance, management and future prospects of the Indian seaports and to trace the impact of private sector participation in the port sector.
4. To assess the likely impact of port restructuring and modernisation in the post-reform era and the key issues and implication of containerisation at the port.
5. To analyse the measures and indicators of port performance and productivity.
6. To analyse port governance.

Data Sources

1. Basic Port Statistics of India (1991 to 2013), published by the Transport Research Division, Ministry of Surface Transport, Government of India, New Delhi.
2. The Data Bank of Indian Ports Association (IPA), New Delhi.
3. *Economic Survey* (various issues), Government of India, Ministry of Finance Economic Division.
4. *Statistical Abstract* (various issues), CSO, Ministry of Statistics and Programme Implementation, New Delhi.
5. *India Yearbook* (1995 to 2015), Publication Division, Ministry of Information and Broadcasting, Government of India.
6. Various issues of *Indian Infrastructure* and the *Link Global Trade & Freight Review*.

Methodology

The following methods have been used to analyse the structure, functions and performance of the major ports of India:

1. To estimate the long-term trends of cargo traffic over time, the qualitative and quantitative changes in the nature of cargo, changes

in the export and import structure and container traffic of the ports whose growth rate has been computed for the period 1990–91 to 2012–13.

2. To test the performance of the ports, a Composite Index has been computed which is a function of the interplay of a number of variables for which a time series data (1990–91 to 2012–13) has been collected for the following indicators:
   (a) *Ship Turn-Round Time* (TRT): It is the total time spent by a ship since its entry till its departure.
   (b) *Pre-Berthing Waiting Time* (PBWT): It means the time for which a ship waits before getting entry into a berth.
   (c) *Non-Working Time at Berth* (NWTB): Non-Working time of a ship is when it goes without loading or unloading of cargo at berth.
   (d) *Output per Ship Berth Day* (OSBD) means the total tonnage handled or distributed over the total number of ship berth days.
   (e) *Cargo Handled* in a year by an individual port.
   (f) *Number of Vessels* in a year by an individual port.

The basic limitation of this method of construction of the Port Performance Index (PPI) is that while combining the performance indicators, it gives subjective adhoc weights to different indicators. To overcome such a problem, all the indicators have been converted into scale free by subtracting the mean value from the real value of each indicator and after dividing them by their respective standard deviation. Finally, all the values have been added to find out the composite index (Z score).

Literature Review

Ports play an important role in the economy of the maritime nations by facilitating foreign trade. They are thus catalysts for social and economic development for any maritime nation. Maritime transportation has been the lifeblood of world trade since time immemorial. Thus, their study becomes very important for understanding the subject matter carefully.

The available literature on the ports and their functioning and performance is vast, hence for convenience it has been grouped under the following themes:

1. Conceptual, historical and contemporary studies.
2. Globalisation and port privatisation.
3. Studies to assess the performance efficiency and productivity of ports.
4. Studies analysing the process of modernisation and development of ports.

Conceptual, Historical and Contemporary Studies

Kidwai (1992)[11] in her work "Conceptual and Methodological Issues: Port Cities and Port-Hinterlands" deals with the basic concepts in port geography like ports, harbours, entrepots, site and situation of ports, stages in the evolution of seaports, port enclaves, outposts, port-hinterlands, forelands, port complexes, port concentration, port diffusion, port cities, etc. According to her, a port is essentially an economic concept; a harbour, a physical one. A *port* is the place of contact where goods and people as well as cultures are transferred between land and maritime space. It is a knot where the oceanic and inland transport lines meet and intervene. A harbour is the sheltered area of deep water. An *entrepot* is essentially a trans-shipment point where the transfer of goods and passengers takes place from ship to ship. According to Kidwai, the origin, evolution and growth of a port depend on many physical and cultural factors. Among the physical factors, the site is the most important. The *site* is the area of land and the associated waters on which the port and the port town are actually developed. *Situation* is a more complicated concept and has both physical and cultural implications. According to her, the most acceptable model for the evolution of ports is the one by Rimmer where he has delineated five stages of port development. She further states that the concept of port-hinterland has become more complex with the passage of time and it is explained as a hierarchy of areas with overlapping layers.

Ray (1993)[12] in his book *Maritime India: Ports and Shipping* has given more weightage to historical and locational aspects for port development and has studied Calcutta as a leading port because of its historical significance.

Fujita and Mori (1995)[13] in their study "Structural Stability and Evolution of Urban System" have explained the evolutionary model of spatial economic development in which there is an interplay between agglomeration economies and the hub-effect of transport nodes in terms of the making of major cities. Their model explains the irreversibility of spatial economic development such as the continuing prosperity of port cities even after the initial advantage of water-access has became irrelevant. It has also been shown that in order to decentralise industries from the core region to the periphery, a temporary protection of industries in the latter by worsening the transport connection with the former for a short period of time may be desirable. But their finding may not be true in case of an economy where ports do not play a decisive role in the growth of the economy.

Beatty and Fothergill (2004)[14] in "Economic Change and the Labour Market in Britain's Seaside Towns" have done a comprehensive study to find out the reasons for the emergence of the seaside town and its potentiality over time in Britain. According to them, the first and most obvious reason is that joblessness in seaside towns is the result of the decline of the traditional tourist base. The second potential explanation for the apparent difficulties is the weakness in the rest of the local economy. A third possibility is that imbalances in the seaside economy reflect in-migration as outstripping jobs. The fourth possibility is a variation on the immigration theme.

Globalisation and Port Privatisation

The Port Policy Report (2001)[15] "Opening up the Sector in Phases" emphasised that the government has taken several policy initiatives to allow joint ventures and foreign collaborations for port development. It has also allowed a 100 per cent FDI in the sector and taken up port corporatisation.

The Port Sector Report (2001)[16] "Coping with Growth" reveals that Indian ports have long been plagued by problems of inefficiency, overmanning and poor management. However, all of these have begun to change with the government encouraging private participation in developing port facilities. The minor ports have succeeded in attracting private interest, but the major ports still have a long way to go.

The report on "Private Participation in Ports: Picking up at Last" (2001)[17] reveals the response to government initiatives for attracting private sector participation in the major ports which has been quite slow. Private participation has been mostly restricted to the licensing of operations of existing container berths or granting BOOT concessions for increasing the terminal capacity. On the other hand, quite a few states have succeeded in involving the private sector in port activities.

The report on "Port Financing: Still a Trickle" (2001)[18] indicates that despite liberalised rules for private participation and several fiscal incentives, uncertainties continue to cloud such crucial issues as the rate of return and the level of comfort available to the banks and Financial Institutions (FIs). In India, the leading domestic FIs in the area of port financing are ICICI, IDBI, IFCI and IDFC. The World Bank's private arm, the International Finance Corporation (IFC), has been an active participant in providing both debt and equity. The Asian Development Bank (ADB) is also a significant player.

Kotak (2001)[19] in his paper, "Privatisation of Ports", has analysed the opportunities and challenges in the privatisation of ports and terminals.

A.J. Baird (2001)[20] in his paper, "Trends in Port Privatisation", seeks to tackle questions such as what is the extent of private sector intervention in the seaports; which specific seaport activities do the public and private sector perform; what methods of privatisation are used; what changes does this imply for the role of both the public and private sector and what are perceived to be the main advantages of these changing institutional arrangements?

The report on "Port Policy and Privatisation (2002)"[21] in the *Indian Infrastructure* deals with the situation in the port sector that has been shrouded in ambiguity for many years. On the one hand, the Major Port Trusts Act was passed in 1963 to permit private participation in the development of port facilities but on the other hand, the environment provided by the successive governments was never really conducive to any sort of activity. In fact, it was as late as October 1996 that the Ministry of Surface Transport finally issued the first comprehensive guidelines on the related issues.

The report on "Major Ports-Performance Round-up (2002)[22], in the *Indian Infrastructure* reveals that India has 12 major ports; out of these Vishakhapatanam leads in terms of cargo traffic. The JNPT is the most advanced in terms of containerisation followed by Chennai. On the privatisation front, the Visakhapatanam and Chennai ports have been in the forefront. Ennore is the first major corporate port of India. In the last few years, in terms of profitable commodities, petroleum/oil/lubricants have overtaken coal as the commodity that earns the maximum revenue for the ports.

Mukherjee (2003)[23] in "A Time to Change" posits that the port sector in general and the major ports in particular now stand at the crossroads. The winds of change are blowing away monolithic monopolies. The evolving environment is one of competitive commercialisation and corporatisation; B.O.T. berths and facilities are already in existence. Foreign ports like the Port of Singapore Authority are now part of the scenario. Private ports are sprouting in the backyards of major ports and existing minor ports are being privatised. The Major Port Trusts Act is being amended. Joint ventures between major ports and other business partners are now trying to come up. The ports, therefore find themselves in a rapidly shifting environment. Liberalisation, privatisation and globalisation are heralding in an era of unprecedented growth in the port sector.

Raman (2004)[24] in "Corporatisation of Ports: Is it the Way Forward?" has addressed the limited issue of the format or structure of moving forward in a dynamic, competitive and complex segment of the infrastructure sector. He attempts an objective analysis of the corporate format of management for the development of the port sector. The Government of India has taken a policy decision to corporatise the major ports in the country. Corporatisation of the other ports is on the anvil. A bill in this regard has been introduced in the Parliament. Presently, it is before the Standing Committee of the Parliament.

Studies to Assess Performance, Efficiency and Productivity of the Ports

In 1976, the United Nations Conference on Trade and Development (UNCTAD)[25] presented a report on "Port Performance Indicators" and advised the port authorities on the collection and use of a set of performance indicators concerning both operational and financial aspects of port operation. The benefits associated with each indicator were discussed to aid in the selection of the indicators for implementation. Indicators had been selected with a view to provide assistance to the port management in medium-term planning and control. From then onwards, the port authorities all over the world seriously thought of the necessity of analysing the importance of operational and financial indicators.

Maffait (1979)[26] in "Port Performance Indicators" described the need for the measures of port performance and inter-port comparison and norms. A number of primary indicators such as berth throughput, ship turn-round time, berth occupancy, productivity and labour costs have been described. In his study, a number of secondary indicators such as the tonnage handled per metre of quay and the over-quay throughputs per metre also have been brought out. A model to study the elements of the turn-round of ships has also been developed.

Kek Choo Chung[27] in his article, "Port Performance Indicators", states that the operational performance of a port is generally measured in terms of the speed with which a vessel is despatched, the retreat with which the cargo is handled and the duration that the cargo stays in the port prior to shipment or post discharge. However, a progressive port manager would also wish to know how extensively and intensively its assets are being utilised as well as how well the operations perform financially. Indicators to measure these performances are determined generally in relation to the tonnage of shipping calling at the port and to the volume of cargo handled since the port services in the main are rendered to the ships and cargo. This note discusses the main indicators used by the ports and for an ease of reference tabulation is presented at the end, which briefly describes how the indicators are determined.

De (1999)[28] in "Performance of Indian Ports" has defined three types of performance indicators such as operational performance indicators, asset performance indicators and financial performance indicators. In his study, the Port Performance Index (PPI) of all the major ports has been calculated and a ranking done based on this index. In his analysis, he concludes that two of the operational performance indicators of Pre-Berthing Waiting Time (PBWT) and Ship Turn-Round Time (TRT) and one asset performance indicator of Berth Occupancy Rate (BOR) became the first three most influential variables in determining the performance of an individual port. Moreover, financial performance indicators like operating Surplus Ton of Cargo Handled (PTOS) and the Rate of Return of Turnover (RRT) have emerged as factors of low importance in determining the performance of an individual port.

Chakraborthy (2000)[29] in "Analysis of Performance of Major Ports during the First Quarter of 1999-2000" has studied the performance of the major ports during the first quarter of 1999–2000. In this study, the ranking of ports was done separately in terms of traffic, absolute growth of traffic, variety of commodity handled, ship traffic, average pre-berthing detention (PBD), average output per ship day and average turn-round time. This study has not considered the ranking of ports based on all the parameters taken together.

Ghosh and De (2001)[30] in "Indian Ports and Globalisation Grounding Economics in Geography" have been concerned with the economics of Indian ports as one of the important phenomena in the Indian economic geography and its relationship with regional development under the free market economy. A PPI derived with the help of the principal component analysis of the eight individual port performance indicators shows that overseas traffic intensity is the most significant determinant of performance. With an increasing openness of the economy and the absence of an integrated policy towards the export transport network, there is a decline in the export intensity and rising domestic coastal traffic in the Indian ports.

Bose (2001)[31] in his article "Cargo Handling of Major Ports in India:

A Case Study" has attempted to analyse the performance of the major ports in India taking into account the absolute cargo handled by them during 1951–52 to 1992–93. The Kolkata-Haldia port is the particular focus for study for the same period, with a view to determine the reasons for its deteriorating performance.

Chakrabarty and Das (2002)[32] in the "Comparison of Performance of Major Ports of India during April to September 2000 through a Single Measure of Efficiency: Few Approaches" have emphasised that the performance of a port is usually reflected by a set of physical/financial indicators viz. cargo throughput, average turn-round time (TRT), average output per ship day, average pre-berthing detention (PBD), cost per tonne etc. In their paper, they have calculated efficiency by an arithmetic mean of the ratios of indicators; the Calculation of weights for Different Indicators and Ports; Efficiency: Weights Proportional to the Share of Ports; Efficiency: Uniform Weights to all Ports, Efficiency by a geometric mean of the ratios of indicators; Efficiency by the volume of Parallelepiped, Efficiency by Inner Product Approach, etc.

Sarkar (2002)[33] in the "Principle of Traffic Forecasting" has emphasised that there are several micro- and macroeconomic variables that determine the actual traffic movement through the particular ports. While the management of a particular port can effectively manage land influence and the microeconomic variables, it has limited ability to influence the macroeconomic factors which depend on the policies of the government and the politics and activities of the maritime trade bodies.

Ramakrishnan (2002)[34] in his study "Indian Ports Performance", reveals the performance of 2000–01 during which the major ports handled 281 MT of cargo, whereas in 1950, five ports had handled 20 MT. The main drawback with the Indian ports is that the ships have to wait to berth and while at berth the handling is largely labour-oriented, resulting in reduced productivity and inefficiency; the Indian ports lacks the zeal and competitive spirit required to attain speed in productivity.

Kumar and Bhasi (2004)[35] in "A Comparative Study of Performance of India Major Sea Ports" have compared the performance of eleven major ports in India. The ranking of the ports is done on the basis of four important performance indicators: (1) Operation Performance (2) Financial Performance (3) Facilities Available (4) Manpower and its utilisation. A weighted score model has been developed by them to rank the ports based on the four performance indicators. According to them, the weights have been chosen on the basis of the opinion of the experts in the field.

Studies Analysing the Process of Modernisation and the Development of Ports

The report on "Port Services: A Fragmented Industry Dominated by a Handful of Operators" (2001)[36] is concerned with the lack of port modernisation and the increased costs of operations. These have emerged as the most serious threats to the domestic litherage and barging industry. Different regulations framed a long time ago—like the Coastal Vessels Act, 1917 pertaining to Goa and Gujarat—fail to cater to the current requirement of the industry. Moreover, a lack of coordination and cooperation amongst the main players and the unorganised nature of the industry have added to the difficulties in the battle for survival.

De and Palit (2001)[37] in the "Impact of Performance on Traffic: Evidence from Major Ports of India" attempt to analyse a new emerging approach to the funding, management and operation of port infrastructure. Governments around the world are improving the operational efficiency of national ports through institutional reform, changing the role of port authorities and increasing the use of private sector. Billions in private capital have been pledged for capacity expansion and service modernisation in the world port system during 1991–98. Although, India has opened the sector for private investments for modernisation and capacity addition, its performance of port system is still hovering around a suboptimal level. In the paper, they have also emphasised that significant port performance can lead to a significant increase in port throughput, which may then increase the demand for port services. Moreover, in explaining this, they have found increasing economies of scale. If ports perform better by primarily improving their operational and asset performance, then their traffic will go up.

Ramakrishnan (2003)[38] in "Scenario of Port Handling and Vision" firmly believes that a port is as an infrastructure which affords the transit facilities of import/export of trade/cargo and is an important infrastructure for socio-economic development. High volume/low value and more than 90 per cent of the import/export trade passes through ports. This article coves issues of port-handling, growth of port traffic, composition of port traffic, predicting the traffic for future development of the ports, economic development, technological and sociological changes, government politics on import/export, industrial development, drought or good rains, lack of infrastructure facilities such as road/rail, port privatisation–port development, increased productivity, better management, flexibility in operation and use of latest equipments.

Ranade[39] in the "Impact of Infrastructure Development on the Ports of India's Western Coast" attempts to analyse the infrastructural development of the ports on the western coast of India. He finds that the infrastructural development on the western coast has had a positive impact on the traffic handled by these ports. After the commissioning of the Konkan Railway, the connectivity of these ports with the other parts of the country has increased. With the improvement in infrastructural facilities for handling the traffic of specialised items like LPG, edible oil, POL products, other liquids, cement, etc., the trade at these ports has become more diversified. The composition of trade is also responsible for the variations in the growth of traffic at the ports. The JNPT with a more diversified composition of cargo has recorded a higher rate of growth as compared to the other ports. The analysis also reveals that the improved connectivity of the western coastal ports after the construction of Konkan Railway has helped to relieve the congestion at the Mumbai Port. The impact of infrastructural development and the upgradation of infrastructure facilities is visible in the increase in the volume of traffic being handled by these ports.

NOTES

1 Kindelberger, C.P. (1996), *World Economic Primacy: 1500-1990*, Oxford Unit Press (OUP), New York.

2 Ray, Animesh *Maritime India: Ports and Shipping*, Pearl Publishers, Kolkata, 1993.
3 Ghosh, Buddhadeb and De, Prabir, "Indian Ports and Globalisation Grounding Economics in Geography", *Economic and Political Weekly*, August 25, 2001, p. 3271.
4 Ramakrishanan, R., Ibid.
5 *Ports of India*, India Infrastructure Publishing Pvt. Ltd., Qutab Institutional Area, New Delhi, table of contents.
6 "Port Financing: Still a Trickle", *Indian Infrastructure*, July 2001, pp. 28-29.
7 "Tariff Authority for Major Ports", *Indian Infrastructure*, June 2004, p. 32.
8 Ghosh, Buddhadeb and De, Prabir, op. cit., p. 2.
9 Kidwai, Atiya and Kuzur, "Seaports, Dry Ports and Development Corridors: Implications for Regional Development in Globalizing India", Working Paper 178, February 2015, Institute for Studies in Industrial Development, New Delhi.
10 Ministry of Shipping, Road Transport & Highways (2013), Government of India.
11 Kidwai, A.K. (1992), "Conceptual and Methodological Issues: Port Cities and Port-Hinterlands" in Indu Banga (ed.), *Ports and Their Hinterlands in India 1700-1950*, Manohar Publications, pp.7-43.
12 Ray, A. (1993), op. cit., p. 1.
13 Fujita, M. and Mori (1995), "Structural Stability and Evolution of Urban System", *Regional Science and Urban Economics*, Vol. 34(8), pp. 41-59.
14 Beatty, Christina and Fothergill, Stephen (2004), "Economic Change and the Labour Market in Britain's Seaside Towns", *Regional Studies*, July, Vol. 38(5), p. 461-480.
15 "Port Policy: Opening Up the Sector in Phases", *Indian Infrastructure*, July 2001, p. 23.
16 "Port Sector: Coping With Growth", *Indian Infrastructure*, July 2001, p. 22.
17 "Private Participation in Ports: Picking Up at Last", *Indian Infrastructure*, July 2001, p. 24.
18 "Port Financing: Still a Trickle", op. cit., 2.
19 Kotak, Krishna (2001), "Privatisation of Ports", *Times Shipping Journal*, Vol. 1(8), pp. 36.
20 Baird, Alfred J. (2001) "Trends in Port Privatisation", *Ports and Harbour*, Jan-Feb, pp. 16-21.
21 "Port Policy and Privatisation", *Indian Infrastructure*, June, 2002, Vol. 4(4), pp. 24-25.
22 "Major Ports: Performance Round-up", *Indian Infrastructure*, June, 2002, pp. 28-30.
23 Mukherjee, S. (2001), "A Time to Change", *Indian Ports*, Vol. 32(3), Jan., pp.17-21.
24 Raman, R. (2004), "Corporatisation of Ports: Is it the Way Forward?", *Indian Ports*, Jan., Vol 35(3), p. 23.
25 UNCTAD Report (1976), "*Port Performance Indicators*", United Nations Conference on Trade and Development at Geneva, United Nations, New York.
26 Maffait, G., "Port Performance Indicators", Proceedings of the UNCTAD/ECA

Seminar on Port Operation, Odessa, USSR, 7-8 August 1978, United Nations, Nov.1979, pp. 173-182.

27 Kek Choo Chung (1993), "Port Performance Indicators", Transport, Water and Urban Development Department, the World Bank.

28 De, Prabir (1999), "Performance of Indian Ports", *Journal of Indian Ports*, Oct., Vol. 31(2), pp. 5-10.

29 Chakraborthy, S. N. (2000), "Analysis of Performance of Major Ports during the First Quarter of 1999-2000", *EXIM Shipping Times*, New Year Special Supplement, pp. 23-34.

30 Ghosh, Buddhadeb and De, Prabir, op. cit., p. 2.

31 Bose, Santu Kumar (2001), "Cargo Handling of Major Ports in India: A Case Study", *Economic and Political Weekly*, August 25, pp. 3284 – 3288.

32 Chakrabarty, S.N. and Das, Rebecca (2002), "Comparison of Performance of Major Ports of India during April to September 2000 through a Single Measure of Efficiency: Few Approaches", *Indian Ports*, Sept., pp. 15-30.

33 Sarkar, J. (2002), "Principle of Traffic Forecasting", *Indian Ports*, July, pp. 9-12.

34 Ramakrishnan, R. (2002), "Indian Ports Performance", *The Link*, Feb., pp. 26-29.

35 Kumar, R. Sasi and Bhasi, M. (2004), "A Comparative Study of Performance of Indian Major Sea Ports" Indian *Ports*, Vol. 36(2), Oct., pp. 9-18.

36 "Port Services: A Fragmented Industry Dominated by a Handful of Operators", *Indian Infrastructure*, July 2001.

37 De, Prabir and Palit, T.K. (2001), "Impact of Performance on Traffic: Evidence from Major Ports of India", *Indian Ports*, Dec., pp. 27-35.

38 Ramakrishanan, R., op. cit., p. 2.

39 Ranade, Prabha Shastri, "Impact of Infrastructure Development on the Ports of India's Western Coast", *Foreign Trade Review*, pp. 69-84.

1

Port Traffic: Composition and Volume

Ports provide an interface between the oceanic and land-based transport. In India, the traffic has traditionally been handled mostly at major ports. However, over the years, non-major ports have also witnessed a significant growth in traffic. The growth in the cargo handled at the Indian ports has increased from a level of 19.38 million tonnes (major ports) in 1950–51 to 913.15 million tonnes (both major and non-major ports) by 2011–12. The share of traffic at the major and non-major ports stood around 560.13 and 353.02 million tonnes, respectively. Approximately, 95 per cent of India's foreign trade by volume and 70 per cent by value is carried on through maritime transport. This underlines the importance of sustaining the growth and development of the port infrastructure for its contribution to the Indian economy. The strengthening of the maritime infrastructure will have a favourable impact on the country's trade front and economic growth.[1]

It is inevitable for Indian ports to have many advantages like an excellent port location close to the international shipping route on the east–west shipping corridor. It requires a minimal maintenance of dredging. It also has a natural water depth of more than 20 metres within a nautical mile off the coast. In the abovementioned milieu, it is imperative to analyse the intra and inter-port cargo handling, composition of the cargo and the major commodities at the major ports of India. One of the major themes of the argument is to search for the causes and determinants of the traffic being handled at the major ports of India. What are the key geographical determinants and their impact on the overall traffic handling at the individual ports, is one of the major apprehensions of the analysis. Very few attempts have been made, both at the theoretical and the analytical levels, to understand the Indian port system, specifically from colonialism to globalism. This study is an attempt to fill some of this lacuna through the analysis of ports as an infrastructural input and in the identification of some of the regional-level issues in port development.

Basic Port Statistics, Ministry of Surface Transport (MOST), Government of India (GOI); Indian Ports Association (IPA) Reports and Publications; Indian Infrastructure Report; Economic Survey and individual port sites have been used for data collection, extraction, computation and compilation.

India is endowed with an extensive coastline of about 7516.6 kilometres, which forms one of the biggest peninsulas in the world. Presently, there are nine coastal states—namely, Gujarat, Maharashtra, Goa, Karnataka, Kerala (on the west coast) and Tamil Nadu, Andhra Pradesh, Orissa, West Bengal (on the east coast). The coastal states have 12 major ports (11 Government and 1 corporate) and approximately 200 notified minor and intermediate ports[2]. India had only five major ports at Kolkata, Mumbai, Chennai, Cochin and Visakhapatnam when it became independent in 1947[3] (Table 1.1). Among these 12 major ports, six are located on the west coast (Kandla, Mumbai, Jawaharlal Nehru Port, Mormugao, New Mangalore and Cochin) and six on the east coast (Tuticorin, Chennai, Ennore, Paradip, Visakhapatanam, and Kolkata). Four of the major ports viz, Kolkata, Mumbai, Chennai and Mormugao are more than 100 years old. The ports of Kandla, Tuticorin, New Mangalore, Haldia and Paradip came into existence after independence. JNPT became operational after 1989. Ennore is the first major corporate port of India which started its operation in 2001. West Bengal is the only maritime state, which, even with an adequate waterfront has no declared minor port.

Table 1.1: Location, Year and Important Functions of the Major Ports of India

Ports	*Year of Est.*	*Location*		*Special Features*
		Lat.	*Long.*	
Kolkata (West Bengal)	1870	22°33′N	88°18′E	A riverine port and impounded docks located on the bank of the Hoogly River. Handles diversified commodities, coming from S.E. Asian countries, Australia and New Zealand.
Mumbai (Maharashtra)	1873	18°54′N	72°49′E	Natural Harbour with impounded Wet Docks, it is the leading general cargo port handling general cargo traffic, trade in containerized cargo and is the leading POL[4].
Chennai (Tamil Nadu)	1881	13°06′N	80°18′E	Artificial Harbour with Wet Docks, it is the oldest artificial harbour on the east coast of India. Handles petroleum products, crude oil, fertilizers, iron ore and dry cargo.
Cochin (Kerala)	1930	9°58′N	76°16′E	Natural harbour (lagoon port); handles the export of tea, coffee and spices and imports of petroleum oil and fertilizers.
Visakhapatnam (Andhra Pradesh)	1933	17°42′N	83°23′E	Natural Harbour; India's deepest landlocked port handling crude oil and petroleum products.[5]
Kandla (Gujarat)	1955	23°01′N	70°13′E	Kandla port is situated in the Kandla Creek (Tidal Creek) and is 90 km. from the mouth of the Gulf Of Kutch. Handles crude oil, petroleum products, edible oil, food grains, salt, cotton, etc.
Mormugao (Goa)	1963	15°25′N	73°47′E	Open Protected Natural Harbour (at the mouth of river Zuari); It is the premier iron ore exporting port of India with an annual throughput of over 18 million tonnes of iron ore traffic. The Port accounts for about half of India's iron ore export and ranks within the first ten leading iron ore exporting ports of the world.[6]
Paradip (Orissa)	1965	20°15′N	86°40′E	Artificial Lagoon Port; handles iron ore and coal.

(Contd.)

Table 1.1 (Contd.)

Ports	*Year of Est.*	*Location*		*Special Features*
		Lat.	*Long.*	
New Mangalore (Karnataka)	1975	12°55′N	74°48′E	Artificial Lagoon Port; handles the export of the iron ore of Kundremukh and the imports of petroleum products, fertilisers, edible oils, etc.
Haldia (West Bengal)	1977	22°02′N	88°06′E	A new port which has been developed on the River Hoogly to relieve the Kolkata port. Also a site of refinery. HDC is the satellite port of the Kolkata port. It provides a functional and operational basis to the main port.
Tuticorin (Tamil Nadu)	1979	8°45′N	78°13′E	Artificial Harbour; handles mainly coal, salt, edible oil, dry cargo and petroleum products.
JNPT (Maharashtra)	1989	18°57′N	72°56′E	All-weather tidal port; equipped with modern facilities having mechanised container over 60 per cent of cargo handling.
Ennore (Tamil Nadu)	2001	13°16′N	80°21′E	Artificial Harbour; first corporatised port of India which started operation since 2001. The Ennore Port is a multifunctional energy port of the New Millennium.

Source: Compiled from the Basic Port Statistics of India, MOST, GOI and various issues of *Indian Ports* and *The Link Global Trade* and *Freight Review*.

1.1 Major Ports: An Overview

A noteworthy feature of the performance of India's port traffic during the years 2002–08 in particular has been its much higher growth compared to the corresponding growth in the world seaborne trade. To a large extent, the strong growth of India's seaborne cargo traffic has reflected buoyancy in India's overall Gross Domestic product (GDP) growth and robust growth in merchandise trade in recent years. As a result, the growth in India's seaborne cargo throughput during 2002–08 outstripped growth in both the world trade and output. In the face of uncertain global market conditions and more challenging domestic market environment, India's seaborne cargo traffic grew by a mere 2.49 per cent in 2008–09 but recovered sharply to 14.27 per cent in 2009–10. Deceleration in the growth of cargo traffic during 2008–09 is attributed to mainly the exogenous factors rooted in the global and domestic growth dynamics.

Table 1.2: Traffic Growth at Major Ports

Year	*Traffic (in Million Tonnes)*	*CAGR (per cent)*
1950-1951	20.10	
1959-1960	31.50	5.12
1969-1970	54.43	5.62
1979-1980	77.59	3.61
1989-1990	147.58	6.64
1999-2000	271.92	6.30
2009-2010	591.09	7.51

Figure 1.1: Traffic Growth at Major Ports

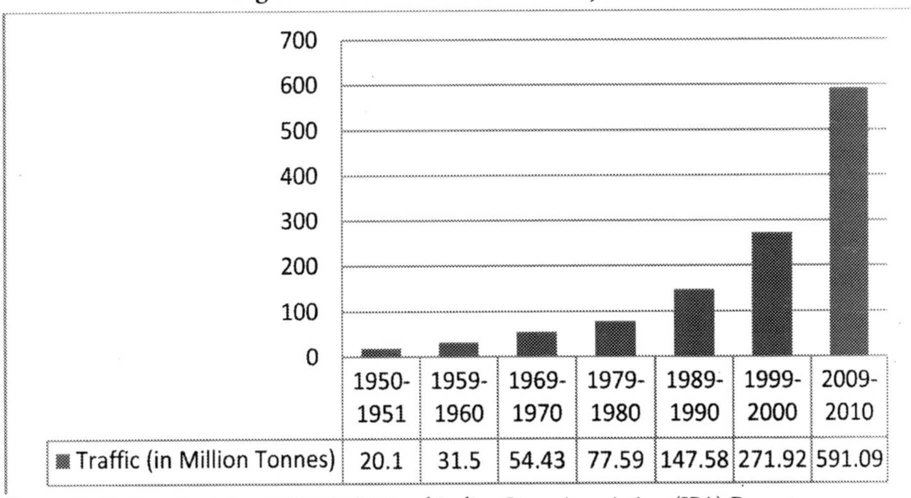

Source: Basic Port Statistics, MOST, GOI and Indian Ports Association (IPA) Report.

In order to realise this growth potential, a number of policy initiatives have been taken during the recent past. Attention has been focused on the improvement in infrastructure, modernisation of existing facilities, better logistic chain, doing away with the licensing system, more openings in the domestic retail market with an entry for the world class players, increased avenues for Special Economic Zone type of projects, etc. In the context of the port sector, the private sector has been allowed in development of Port Infrastructure; new berths are being commissioned on a BOT basis. The documentation procedures have become simple. To become globally competitive, utmost importance has been placed on development of physical infrastructure like roads, airports, seaports, railways in general and the port sector in particular. A single-window concept with a web-based Port Community System has been introduced in many ports. The Indian ports—earlier developed to handle bulk and break bulk cargo—are now developing more containerised handling facilities. The development of an International Container Transhipment terminal at Cochin is in the offing. Due to concerted efforts over the years, the Jawaharlal Nehru and Chennai ports are attracting a larger number of mother vessels for the containers.

1.2 Major Ports: Port Traffic

The major ports have witnessed ups and downs in the growth pattern of traffic during the last five decades, but the thirst for upsurge in achieving the new heights in traffic handling is still continuing. The overall Compound Annual Rate of Growth (CAGR) of traffic at the major ports during 1950–51 to 2009–10 has been 5.80 per cent, whereas during the post-liberalisation period i.e. from 1991–92 to 2009–10, the CAGR was 7.31 per cent. If the CAGR of traffic growth at the major ports is taken into consideration for the last five years, it has been 7.28 per cent, whereas it is 10.73 per cent if the traffic is taken for the three years before the global economic recession period i.e. 2008–09 and 2009–10, which is the highest growth rate since 1960. Cargo traffic at 561.09 million tonnes at India's 12 major ports during 2009–10 accounted for around two-thirds of India's total seaborne cargo (849.9 million tonnes) and showed an improvement in growth to 5.80 per cent in 2009–10, compared to a 2.2 per cent increase in 2008–09. The total cargo of 561.09 million tonnes comprised the cargo loaded, cargo unloaded and transhipped to the tune of 322.6 million tonnes, 211.0 million tonnes and 26.6 million tonnes, respectively (Table 1.2).

The analysis of the cargo handled at the 12 major ports reveals that the Paradip Port posted the highest increase by 22.8 per cent, followed by Mormugao (17.2 per cent), Cochin (14.5 per cent), Kandla (10.1 per cent), Tuticorin (8.1 per cent), Chennai (6.2 per cent), JNPT (6.1 per cent), Mumbai (5.1 per cent), Kolkata Dock System (5 per cent) and Vishakhapatnam (2.5 per cent). The Paradip Port accounted for a share of 10.2 per cent in the total cargo handled by the major ports but contributed more than one-third of the incremental traffic handled at the major ports in the country during 2009–10.

Table 1.3: Growth of Traffic at the Major Ports

Year	*No. of Major Port*	*Traffic (Million Tonnes)*	*per cent Increase*
1950	5	19.20	
1960	6	39.90	51.88
1970	8	55.80	28.49
1980	10	81.30	31.37
1990	11	153.90	47.17
2000	11	271.20	43.25
2001	12	281.00	3.49
2002	12	287.70	2.33
2003	12	363.00	20.74
2004	12	390.00	6.92
2005	12	383.75	-1.63
2006	12	423.56	9.40
2007	12	463.78	8.67
2008	12	519.31	10.69
2009	12	530.53	2.11
2010	12	561.09	5.45
2011	12	570.03	1.57
2012	12	560.15	-1.76

Source: Basic Port Statistics, MOST, GOI and Indian Ports Association (IPA) Report.

Table 1.4: Cargo Traffic at Major Ports
(During 1991–92 to 2011–12)

Port Name	2011-12			2008-09			2003-04			1996-97			1991-92		
	Traffic in MT	*per cent of total*	*Rank*	*Traffic in MT*	*per cent of total*	*Rank*	*Traffic in MT*	*per cent of total*	*Rank*	*Traffic in MT*	*per cent of total*	*Rank*	*Traffic in MT*	*per cent of total*	*Rank*
Visakhapatanam	67.42	12.04	2	63.91	12.05	2	47.74	13.85	1	34.5	15.18	1	21	10.02	4
Kolkata	43.24	7.72	7	54.22	10.22	5	41.05	11.9	3	23.12	10.17	4	16.1	16.14	5
Chennai	55.71	9.95	5	57.49	10.84	3	36.71	10.65	4	31.85	14.01	3	25.05	3.34	2
Kandla	82.50	14.73	1	72.23	13.61	1	41.52	12.04	2	33.73	14.84	2	21.52	12.78	3
Mumbai	56.18	10.03	4	51.88	9.78	6	29.92	8.68	6	33.73	14.84	2	26.26	5.28	1
New Mangalore	32.94	5.88	9	36.69	6.92	9	26.67	7.74	8	12.45	5.48	6	8.27	1.34	7
JNPT	65.75	11.74	3	57.29	10.80	4	31.27	9.07	5	8.07	3.55	10	2.79	4.79	11
Mormugao	39.00	6.96	8	41.68	7.86	8	27.87	8.08	7	17.31	7.62	5	16	19.02	6
Paradip	54.25	9.68	6	46.41	8.75	7	25.31	7.34	9	11.58	5.1	8	7.3	12.96	9
Tuticorin	28.11	5.02	10	22.01	4.15	10	13.68	3.96	10	9.18	4.04	9	5.87	4.53	10
Cochin	20.09	3.59	11	15.23	2.87	11	13.57	3.93	11	11.74	5.17	7	7.48	9.81	8
Ennore	14.96	2.67	12	11.50	2.17	12	9.28	2.69	12						
All Ports	560.15	100.00		530.54	100.00		344.59	100		227.26	100		157.64	100	

Source: Basic Port Statistics, MOST, GOI and Indian Ports Association (IPA) Report.

Table 1.5: Comparative Position of the Major Ports (1991–2012) (Based on the Cargo Handled)

Improved	*Static*	*Decline*
Kandla	Paradip	Kolkata
Visakhapatnam	Tuticorin	Chennai
JNPT	Cochin	Mumbai
Ennore		Mormugao
		New Mangalore

Source: Prepared on the basis of Table 1.4.

Figure 1.2: Cargo Traffic at Major Ports (During 1991-92 to 2011-12)

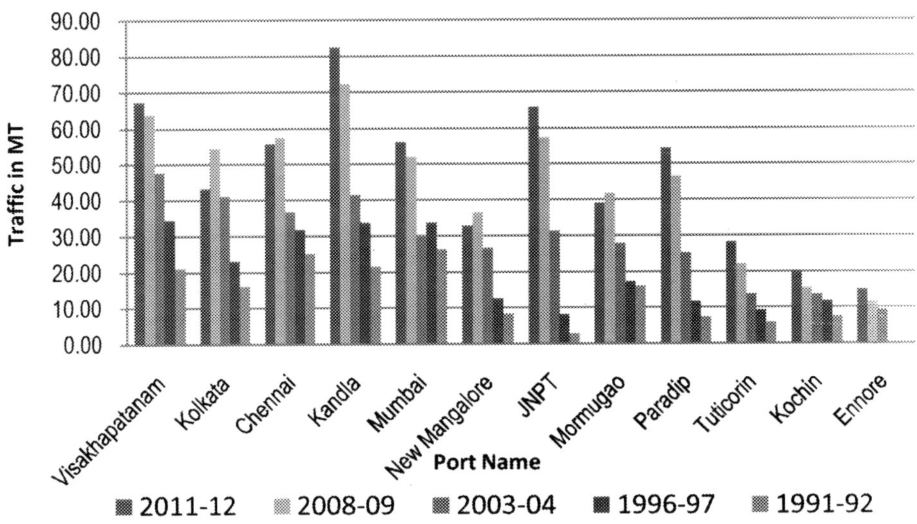

Source: Basic Port Statistics, MOST, GOI and Indian Ports Association (IPA) Report.

1.3 Profiles of the Major Ports of India

1.3.1 Kolkata Dock System (KDS)

The Port of Kolkata is a riverine port in the city of Kolkata, India. The Kolkata Port was set up by the British East India Company after it received trading rights from the Mughal emperor Aurangzeb. It is the oldest operating port in India, having originally been constructed by the British East India Company. Following the shift of power from the company to the British crown, a Port Commission was set up in 1870. Though the port was conceived to be a commercial port and gateway to eastern India, it played a very important role in the Second World War. It was bombed twice by the Japanese forces. After Independence, the Commissioners for the Port of Kolkata were responsible for the port till January 1975 when the Major Port Trusts Act, 1963 came into force. The Port is now run by a Board of Trustees having representatives from the Government, trade bodies, various port users, labour unions and some nominated members.[7]

The Port has two distinct dock systems; Kolkata Docks at Kolkata and a deep-water dock at the Haldia Dock Complex, Haldia. In the nineteenth century, the Kolkata Port was the premier port in British India. After Independence its importance decreased because of the Partition of Bengal (1947), reduction in size of the port hinterland and economic stagnation in eastern India. It has a vast hinterland comprising the entire Eastern India including West Bengal, Bihar, Jharkhand, Uttar Pradesh, Madhya Pradesh, Assam, the North-East Hill States and the two landlocked neighbouring Countries namely, Nepal and Bhutan.

The journey of the Port continues through the tortuous process of ebb and tide, expectancy and despair, intricately woven with the varying draft/ siltation of the river Hooghly, as it continues to adapt and re-engineer itself in newer locales and functions. Kolkata, the first Major Port of India, was once the premier port of the country but since 1966–67 faced a steady decline in its fortunes being relegated to the third, fourth, fifth and sixth positions. However, due to categorical efforts, there had been a steady flourish in cargo and vessel handling and in different spheres of the Port activity from 2004–05 to 2007–08; the Port was positioned in the second and third slots respectively, competing with the other seaports of the country. There prevailed a moderate decline since 2008–09 with some adverse geomorphological changes in the river regime, a general economic downturn and a flight of POL Crude cargo to a neighbouring port. In 2010–11, the port handled 47.545 million tonnes of cargo with the distinction of handling the highest number of vessels. The Port stood third both in Coking Coal and Container Handling and also had the distinction of having registered the highest growth of POL traffic (15.26 per cent) amongst the Indian Major Ports.[8]

1.3.2 Paradip Port Trust

The Paradip Port is an artificial, deep-water port on the East coast of India in the Jagatsinghpur district of Odisha. It is situated at a confluence of the Mahanadi River and the Bay of Bengal. It is situated 210 nautical miles south of Kolkata and 260 nautical miles north of Visakhapatnam. The port is administered by the Paradip Port Trust (PPT), an autonomous corporation wholly owned by the Government of India. The foundation stone for the Paradip Port was laid on 3 January 1962. The Government of India took over the management of the port from the State Government on 1 June 1965. The Government of India declared the Paradip Port Trust as the eighth major port in India on 18 April 1966, making it the first major port on the eastern coast commissioned in independent India. The port is spread over an area of over 7,000 acres (28 km^2). The port operates an autonomous railway system, with its own railway station. It has an 82 kilometres of track length with over 25 sidings for handling cargo. The rail system connects to the Eastern Railways network of the Indian Railways over a 10 km route. The NH 5A is a four-lane national highway connecting the port to Haridaspur near Cuttack, and to the rest of India's highway network.[9]

Paradip Port is one of the Major Ports of India serving the eastern and central parts of the country. Its hinterland extends to the States of Odisha, Jharkhand, Chhattisgarh, West Bengal, Madhya Pradesh and Bihar. The Port mainly deals with bulk cargo apart from other clean cargoes. There has been an unprecedented growth in the traffic handled at this Port in the last decade. The Port has got an ambitious expansion programme to double its capacity in order to meet the ever-increasing demand.

The Paradip Port Trust is one of the premier maritime gateways on the east coast of India based on its core strengths: deep draft, proximity to rich mineral reserves, vicinity to the large hinterland and landlocked regions. The Port is all set to become a hub of the east coast and economic thrust engine for Eastern India by offering world-class cost effective marine and operational services and by leveraging on the highly mechanised and dedicated handling facilities, superior supply chain connectivity and strategic partnerships with private investors. The Port has made an unprecedented growth of traffic from 0.067 million tonnes in the year 1966–67 to 54.25 million tonnes in 2011–12. During the last eight years, the port has expanded its scale and scope of operation for doubling its traffic.[10]

The Port has handled 54.25 million tonnes of cargo during the year 2011–12 in spite of the global economic slowdown and shrinkage of export. The shortfall of 1.78 million tonnes of cargo handled during the year is mainly due to a slump in iron ore exports to the tune of 7.30 million tonnes. The performance parameters on which the efficiency of a Port is measured have improved significantly during the year. The average pre-berthing waiting time, average turn-round time, and average berthday output have improved by 53 per cent, 4 per cent and 12 per cent, respectively, over the corresponding figures of the previous year. Induced by the exponential growth in demand on the existing facilities of the Port, the Management is undertaking various projects to augment capacity and to diversify the operations further to sustain its competitive advantages over all the other Ports.[11]

1.3.3 Visakhapatnam Port Trust

The Port of Visakhapatnam is one of the leading major ports of India. The Port has three harbours viz., outer harbour, inner harbour and the fishing harbour. The outer harbour with a water spread of 200 hectares has 6 berths and the inner harbour with a water spread of 100 hectares has 18 berths. The Port has ambitious plans for modernisation with the vision to become the most preferred Port in the South Asian Region. Considerable investments through the PPP mode are on the anvil, envisaging a deepening of channels and berths, construction of new berths, installation of state-of-art mechanised handling facilities and other logistics. The major thrust areas of development include the deepening of channels, construction of berths, modernisation of cargo handling equipments/systems, connectivity and other logistics.[12]

It is India's second largest port by the volume of the cargo handled. It is located on the east coast of India and is located midway between the Chennai and Kolkata Ports. Although the need for building a port on the east coast to access the Central Provinces was felt by the British in the nineteenth century, the proposal of Col H. Cartwright Reid of the British Admiralty for constructing a harbour at Visakhapatnam was approved by the Government only after the First World War. The inner harbour was built by the Bengal Nagpur Railway between 1927 and 1933 to facilitate the export of manganese ore from the Central Provinces.

During the Second World War, the military significance of the port increased. After India's independence, the port witnessed growth under the various Five Year Plans. Over time, the port has grown from one with 3 berths handling 1.3 lakh tonnes per annum to one with 24 berths and an annual traffic of 65 million tonnes. The port was notified as a major port in 1964 under the Major Port Trusts Act, 1963. Under the Act, the Visakhapatnam Port Trust was given the charge of running the port.

The hinterland of the Visakhapatnam Port extends to Telengana and north-eastern Andhra Pradesh, Chhattisgarh, south-eastern Madhya Pradesh, southern Orissa and the Vidarbha region of Maharashtra. Iron ore, manganese ore, steel products, general cargo, coal and crude oil are the main commodities being handled at this port.

The Visakhapatnam Port is undergoing a modernisation and expansion programme aimed at increasing its capacity. The inauguration of the Gangavaram Port, located 15 km away from the Visakhapatnam Port, has led to a significant diversion of traffic away from the Visakhapatnam Port. This loss of cargo traffic is an important reason for the Port's fall from its position as the largest port in India. The Rashtriya Ispat Nigam Limited (RINL) which runs the Vizag Steel Plant, shifted base to the new Port, taking with it a large chunk of the coal and iron ore traffic. The Visakhapatnam Port is now modernising its coal-handling berth in the outer harbour to enable it to handle cape-size vessels. This will also solve the problem of air pollution caused by the open handling of coal that had earlier led to citywide protests.

As part of its modernisation programme, the Port is also upgrading its general cargo berth in the outer harbour, deepening its inner harbour entrance channel. There are also plans to relocate the fishing harbour at the Port to allow for the expansion of berths and stacking areas and a dredging of the outer harbour is also being undertaken to increase the draft of the main channel to 21 metres.

1.3.4 Ennore Port Limited

The Ennore Port, located on the Coromondel Coast about 24 km north of the Chennai Port, is the 12th major port of India, and the first port in India which is a public company. The Port was declared as a major port under the Indian Ports Act, 1908 in March 1999 and incorporated as the Ennore Port Limited under the Companies Act, 1956 in October 1999. The Ennore Port is the only corporatised major port and is registered as a company. The Ennore Port has been designed as Asia's energy port and envisaged as being a satellite port in order to decongest and improve the environmental quality at the bustling Chennai Port. Designed as a world-class port, it has the capacity to develop 20 berths for handling a variety of bulk, liquid, automobile and container cargo. The Port is an artificial one with features including all-weather, round-the-clock operations, a large back-up land, eco-friendly environment, state-of-the-art navigational facilities, well-organised logistics systems and transport interface.[13]

The Ennore Port was originally conceived for primarily handling thermal coal to meet the requirement of the Tamil Nadu Electricity Board (TNEB) and was endowed with large chunks of land (about 2,000 acres). The scope was expanded taking into account subsequent developments such as the plan of the Government of Tamil Nadu to set up a 1,880 MW LNG power project in association with a private consortium, a large petrochemical park and a naphtha cracker plant.

Commissioned in 2001 and operating on a landlord port concept, it is outsourcing all services required for operation and maintenance, and new terminals are being developed with the participation of the private sector. During the years 2010–11, it handled a total cargo of 11.01 million tonnes. The Port has effectively taken over all the ore movement from the Chennai Port.

The Port has adequate road and rail links. It has obtained an in-principle approval from the Southern Railways for providing rail connectivity to the coal and iron ore stack yards. The Ennore Port Limited (EPL) is also developing an 8-lane Northern Express Road, which would link the Port with the National Highway No. 5. It has a 560 metre (1,840 ft) long coal wharf for berthing two Panamax-size vessels and fully mechanised systems for handling 16 million tonnes of cargo in a year.

1.3.5 Chennai Port Trust

Situated on the Coromandel Coast in south-east India, the Port of Chennai has more than 100 years of tradition. Strategically located and well connected with the major parts of the world, it is today the hub port on the Indian subcontinent. Continuous modernisation, efficient services at a minimum cost, simple and integrated procedures and a user-friendly approach are major attractive forces of this Port. Being the third oldest port among the 12 major ports of India, it is over 125 years old, although maritime trade had started away back in 1639 on the seashore. It is an artificial and all-weather port with wet docks. It was a major travel port before becoming a major container port. It is a substantial reason for the economic growth of Tamil Nadu, especially for the manufacturing boom in South India, and has contributed in no small measure to the development of the city. It is due of the existence of the Port that the city of Chennai became known as the *Gateway of South India*. The Port has become a hub port for containers, cars and project cargo on the east coast of India. From handling a meagre volume of cargo in the early years, consisting chiefly of imports of oil and motors and the export of groundnuts, granite and ores, the Port has moved towards handling 60 million tonnes of cargo in the recent years.

From 1881 to 1945, the cargo handled in the Madras port varied from 0.5 million tonnes to 1 million tonnes. By 1979–80, the traffic touched 10 million tonnes and increased to 15 million tonnes in 1984–85. By 1991–92, the volume was 25 million tonnes, touching 41 million tonnes in 2000–01. Though there was a slump in the next three years, mainly due to the transfer of about 9 million tonnes of thermal coal to the Ennore Port, the Port recovered to handle 47.25 million tonnes in 2005–06. In 2009–10, it handled 61.06 million tonnes of cargo against 57.49 million tonnes in 2008–09 marking an increase of 6.20 per cent and has set a target to handle 75 million tonnes in 2011–12. In 2010–11, the Port handled 61.46 million tonnes; a 0.66 per cent increase over the previous fiscal year. The Port handles a variety of cargo including iron ore, coal, granite, fertilisers, petroleum products, containers, automobiles and several other types of general cargo items.

After commissioning of the iron ore handling capacity at Ennore in the year 2010–11, the iron ore traffic of Chennai Port is expected to be shifted to the Ennore Port and the existing iron ore berth to be converted as a container terminal.

1.3.6 V.O. Chidambaram Port Trust

The V.O. Chidambaram Port Trust, formerly the Tuticorin Port Trust, is one of the 12 major ports in India. It was declared to be a major port on 11 July 1974. Tuticorin has been a centre for maritime trade and pearl fishery for more than a century. A natural harbour with a rich hinterland activated the development of the Port initially with wooden piers and an iron screw pile pier and with connections to the railways. Tuticorin was declared as a minor anchorage port in 1868. It is the second largest port in Tamil Nadu and the fourth largest container terminal in India. The V.O. Chidambaram Port is an artificial port. This is the third international port in Tamil Nadu and its second all-weather port. It has services to USA, China, Europe, Sri Lanka and the Mediterranean countries.[14]

To cope with the increasing trade through Tuticorin, the Government of India sanctioned the construction of an all-weather port there; it brings the second largest revenue through ports to India. On 11 July 1974, the newly constructed Tuticorin Port was declared as the tenth major port. On 1 April 1979, the erstwhile Tuticorin minor port and the newly constructed Tuticorin major port were merged and the Tuticorin Port Trust was constituted under the Major Port Trusts Act of 1963.

During the financial year 2010–11, the Port has handled its highest-ever volume of 25.73 million tonnes, which is 8.15 per cent higher than the volume handled during the previous fiscal. The Port currently handles seven per cent of the total container traffic in India and is an important reason for investment in the southern districts of Tamil Nadu. The Tuticorin Port has the potential to be an international container trans-shipment hub given its unique geographical location. The activity at the port has grown at a rate of 17 per cent per year over the last five years.[15] A large portion of the operations in the Port has been privatised, including handling at the first container terminal.

The Port is also helping to increase tourism in the region. A new ferry has been commenced between Tuticorin and Colombo. Tuticorin is the only port in South India to provide a direct weekly container service to the United States. The transit time to the United States is 22 days. There are regular weekly direct services to Europe (transit time—17 days), China (transit time—10 days) and Red Sea Ports (transit time—8 days). The Port Management with the support of the Ministry of Shipping, Government of India, has achieved a number of key milestones like the launching of the Passenger Ferry Service between Tuticorin and Colombo, the creation of a Cargo Handling Division by a merger of the labour pool with the Port, the completion of the capital dredging project, etc.

1.3.7 Cochin Port Trust

The Cochin Port is a major port on the Arabian Sea–Indian Ocean sea-route and is one of the largest ports in India. The Port lies on two islands in the Lake of Kochi—Willingdon Island and Vallarpadam—towards the Fort Kochi river mouth opening into the Arabian Sea. The International Container Transshipment Terminal (ICTT), part of the Cochin Port, is the largest container trans-shipment facility in India. The port is governed by the Cochin Port Trust (CPT), a Government of India establishment. The modern port was established in 1926 and has completed 86 years of active service.[16]

The Cochin Port is one of a line of maritime-related facilities based in the port-city of Kochi. The others are the Cochin Shipyard, the largest shipbuilding as well as maintenance facility in India; the SPM (single point mooring) facility of the Kochi Refineries, an offshore crude carrier mooring facility; and the Kochi Marina.

The Cochin Port was formed naturally due the great floods in the Periyar in 1341 AD, which choked the Muziris port (Kodungallur), one of the greatest ports in the ancient world. Since then, Cochin became one of the major ports of the world with extensive trading relations with the Romans, Greeks and Arabs—all lured by the traditional spice wealth of the state. The Port further attracted European colonialists like the Portuguese, the Dutch and finally the British who extended their supremacy over the Kochi Kingdom and the port city of Fort Kochi. The traditional port was near Mattancherry (which still continues as the Mattancherry Wharf).

The need of a modern port was first felt by Lord Willingdon during his governorship of the Madras Province of British India. The opening of the Suez Canal made several ships pass near the west coast and he felt the necessity of a modern port in the southern part. He selected the newly-joined Sir Robert Bristow who was a leading British harbour engineer with an extensive experience in maintenance of the Suez Canal. Bristow took charge as the Chief Engineer of the Kochi Kingdom's Port Department in 1920. Since then, he and his team became actively involved in making a Greenfield port. After studying the sea currents, observing tidal conditions and conducting experiments, he was convinced about the feasibility of developing Cochin. He believed that Cochin could become the safest harbour if the ships were to enter the inner channel.

In 1932, the Maritime Board of British India declared the Port of Cochin as a major port. The Port was opened to all vessels up to 30 feet draught. During World War II, the Port was taken over by the Royal Navy to accommodate military cruisers and warships. It was returned to the civil authorities on 19 May 1945. After Independence, the Port was taken over by the government of India. In 1964, the administration of the Port got vested in a Board of Trustees under the Major Port Trusts Act. The cargo handled at the Cochin Port was 20.09 MT in 2011–12; with that, it stands out at the 11th position amongst the 12 major ports of India.

1.3.8 New Mangalore Port Trust

The New Mangalore Port is a modern all-weather port situated at Panambur, Mangalore on the west coast of India, 170 nautical miles south of Mormugao and 191 nautical miles north of the Cochin Port. The Mangalore Harbour Projects, started in 1962, was completed in May 1974.[17] The New Mangalore Port was declared as the ninth Major Port on 4 May 1974. At NMPT, the year 2003–04 has witnessed a considerable improvement in the performance indicators like pre-berthing delay, turn-round-time, berthday output, average output per gang per shift, etc.

The port serves the hinterland of the Karnataka state and to some extent, the state of Kerala. The major commodities exported through the port are iron ore concentrates and pellets, iron ore fines, manganese, granite stones, coffee, cashew and containerised cargo. The major imports of the port are crude and petroleum products, LPG, wood pulp, timber logs, finished fertilisers, liquid ammonia, phosphoric acid, other liquid chemicals, containerised cargo, etc. The port has handled 32.94 MT of cargo in 2011–12.[18]

1.3.9 Mormugao Port Trust

Mormugao is a sub-district and municipal council in the South Goa district in the state of Goa. It is Goa's main port. Ever since it was accorded the status of a Major Port in 1963, the Mormugao port has contributed immensely to the growth of maritime trade in India. It is the leading iron ore exporting port of India with an annual throughput of around 27.33 million tonnes of iron ore traffic.

As the importance of one of India's best natural harbours grew more apparent, Mormugão, which the British called Marmagoa, became a key trading point. It was chosen for the terminus of the new metre gauge railway linking the Portuguese colony to British India. For a fabulous price, the Western India Portuguese Guaranteed Railways Company, a British enterprise, modernised the port and built the railway. Both were opened to the public in July 1886. Mormugao's city of Vasco da Gama was planned and built in the early years of the twentieth century. A colorful city of officials, traders and migrant labourers, it had its Portuguese academies and British club life for several decades.[19]

Mormugao Port, one of the oldest ports on the west coast of India, with a fine natural harbour, has been relentlessly serving the nation in its economic development for over a century. The Mormugao Port is the premier iron ore exporting Port of India with an annual throughput of around 39 million tonnes of traffic. Though ore is the predominant cargo, there has been a steady increase in liquid bulk and general cargo traffic ever since it joined the ranks of the Major Ports of India. Excellent facilities, high productivity, streamlined administration and a dedicated workforce all go towards the making of this Port one of the most efficient ports in the Indian subcontinent. The iron exported through Mormugao constitutes 39 per cent of the total iron ore exports from India, and the port occupies a prestigious position amongst the Major Ports of the country. A major growth has been projected in respect of iron ore, POL and coal traffic.[20]

1.3.10 Nhava Sheva/Jawaharlal Nehru Port Trust (JNPT)

Nhava Sheva is located near Navi Mumbai, on the Konkan mainland across the island city of Mumbai. Spread over 10 square kilometres (2,500 acres), it was developed to relieve pressure on the Mumbai Port. It was inaugurated on 26 May 1989. It is one of the largest ports in the world. The construction of the Nhava Sheva Port was originally planned in 1965. The original plan envisioned the use of the Port for importing foodgrains. Following the Green Revolution in India, India gained a vast surplus in the foodgrain production capacity, so the plans for the Port shifted focus to container traffic. The Nhava Sheva Port is run by the Jawaharlal Nehru Port Trust, an autonomous corporation wholly owned by the Government of India.[21]

Nhava Sheva is well connected to the major highways and rail networks in India. The closest suburban railheads are CBD Belapur and Panvel. The port handles 65 per cent of India's container traffic and has an average berthing period of 37 hours which is very long and inefficient. The expansion plans for the Port include new and extensive terminal access points and connecting roads. The JNPT Container Terminal is operated by the JNPT.

Major exports from the Nhava Sheva are textiles, sporting goods, carpets, textile machinery, boneless meat, chemicals and pharmaceuticals. The main imports are chemicals, machinery, plastics, electrical machinery, vegetable oils and aluminium and other non-ferrous metals. The Port handles cargo traffic mostly originating from or destined for Maharashtra, Madhya Pradesh, Gujarat, Karnataka, as well as most of North India.

The JNPT handled 65.75 million tonnes of total cargo during the financial year 2011–12, which is an all-time record for it. The containerised cargo was 58.25 million tonnes and liquid cargo was 6.66 million tonnes and the remaining 0.84 million tonnes was of dry bulk and break bulk. The JNPT handled 64.32 million tonnes of total cargo during the financial year 2010–11 as against 60.76 million tonnes of cargo handled during the financial year 2009–10. The growth in total traffic during the financial year 2010–11 was 5.85 per cent over that of the previous year.[22] The containerised cargo was 56.43 million tonnes (87.73 per cent); liquid cargo was 6.81 million tonnes (10.58 per cent) and the remaining 1.09 million tonnes (1.69 per cent) was of miscellaneous types of dry bulk cargo (cement), break bulk cargo and vehicles[23].

1.3.11 Mumbai Port Trust

The Mumbai Port has long been the principal gateway to India and has played a pivotal role in the development of the national economy, trade and commerce, as well as the prosperity of the Mumbai city in particular. The Port is administered by the Mumbai Port Trust (MbPT), an autonomous corporation wholly owned by the Government of India. The port is primarily used for bulk cargo, while most container traffic is directed to the Nhava Sheva Port. The Mumbai Harbour has been used by the ships and boats for centuries. It was used by the Maratha Navy, as well as the British and Portuguese colonial navies. The first of the present-day docks of the Mumbai Port were built in the 1870s. The Bombay Port Trust (BPT) was established as a corporation on 26 June 1873. The BPT's founding chairman was Colonel J.A. Ballard. Over the decades, the Port underwent tremendous expansion, with the addition of berths and cargo-handling capacities.[24]

The Port has achieved this position through a continuous endeavour to serve the changing needs of the maritime trade. Though traditionally designed to handle general cargo, over the years, the port has adapted to the changing shipping trends and cargo packaging from break bulk to unitisation/palletisation and containerisation. Besides, it has also developed specialised berths for handling POL and chemicals. For decades, the Mumbai Port was India's premier port.[25] Even today, with the development of the other ports, it caters to a 10 per cent of the country's seaborne trade handled by the Major Ports of the country in terms of volume. It caters to about 19 per cent of the POL traffic handled by the Major Ports.[26]

Having weathered and survived many a change in maritime trade in its long history, the Mumbai Port is today facing challenges posed by competition from the adjoining ports and private ports, changing traffic patterns, inherent physical constraints and the continuing labour-intensive operations, etc. However, the Mumbai Port is taking various measures to render cost-effective and quality services to trade.

1.3.12 Kandla Port Trust

Kandla is a seaport in the Kutch District of the state of Gujarat in western India, near the city of Gandhidham. Located on the Gulf of Kutch, it is one of major ports on the west coast. Kandla was constructed in the 1950s as the chief seaport serving western India, after the partition of India from Pakistan left the port of Karachi in Pakistan.[27] The British Royal India Navy first appraised the Kandla stream in 1851 for suitability as a port; however, it did not conduct a detailed survey until 1922. The Port of Kandla was created in 1931 with a single pier by the erstwhile ruler of Kutch, Khengarji III, who personally identified the spot and also connected the port by extending the lines of the Kutch State Railway from Anjar. When the Port of Karachi was lost to Pakistan, maritime trade in the area shifted to the Port of Mumbai (formerly Bombay). Mumbai's facilities were soon strained beyond capacity. In early 1948, the Indian government created the West Coast Major Port Development Committee to study the feasibility of building a major seaport to replace the Port of Karachi. The Committee recommended locating a port at Kandla.[28]

The Port of Kandla was declared a Major Port in April 1955. The Kandla Port Trust was created by law in 1963 to manage the new port. In 1998, a severe tropical cyclone hit the Port. The official death toll was 1,000 but the locals in the area believed it to be much higher. Most of the casualties were from the illegal immigrant workers in the Port itself and the poor shanty towns in the region.[29]

The Port of Kandla Special Economic Zone (KASEZ) was the first special economic zone to be established in India and in Asia. Established in 1965, the Port of Kandla SEZ is the biggest multiple-product SEZ in the country. Covering over 310 hectares, the special economic zone is just nine km from the Port of Kandla. Today, the Port of Kandla is India's hub for exporting grains and importing oil and one of the highest-earning ports in the country. The major imports entering the Port of Kandla are petroleum, chemicals, and iron and steel and iron machinery; but, it also handles salt, textiles, and grain.

Kandla is the premium port of India. Cargo handling was 82.50 MT in 2011–12, which is the maximum tonnage handling by any major port of India. Kandla has overtaken Vishakhapatnam, which has been the number one port for decades. The growth of cargo traffic at the Kandla Port is associated with the economic development of Gujarat as well as an overhauling of the port infrastructure.[30]

1.3.13 Port Blair Port Trust

The latest addition to the Major Ports was Port Blair on June 2010; the 13th port in the country. Under the Indian Ports Act, 1908, the Government declared the Port Blair Port with its territorial jurisdiction over all the ports of Andaman & Nicobar Islands, as a Major Port w.e.f. 1 June 2010. All major provisions of the Major Port Trusts Act, 1963 have become applicable to the major port of Port Blair from 1 June 2010. With this, the Port Blair Port became the 13th major port of the country. However, within a year of its inception, it was de-notified from the status of major port. It could not meet the requirements of a major port; also, there were many operational issues behind the functioning of the port.

1.4 Non-Major Ports: An Overview

There are 187 non-major ports situated along the peninsular coastline and Sea Islands. These ports are located in the maritime states of Gujarat, Maharashtra, Goa, Karnataka, Kerala, Tamil Nadu, Andhra Pradesh, Orissa,

West Bengal and the Union Territories of Puducherry, Daman & Diu and Lakshadweep. Out of these ports, only a few ports are well-developed and provide all-weather berthing facilities for cargo handling. In 2008–09, only 60 Ports (including the ports of the Andaman & Nicobar Islands) were reported to have handled cargo traffic.

Non-major ports in India collectively handled 288.80 million tonnes of traffic during the year 2009–10 as compared to 87.37 million tonnes of cargo handled in 2000–01. The Cumulative Annual Growth Rate (CAGR) growth in traffic during 2000–01 to 2009–10 achieved by the non-major ports was 14.2 per cent as compared to 9.7 per cent achieved by all the ports in the country. The share of cargo traffic of the non-major ports in the total cargo traffic handled by all the ports in India increased from 10.9 per cent in 2000–01 to 34 per cent in 2009–10. This trend definitely shows the level of competition which the Major Ports have faced during the last few years and is likely to continue in the years to come and as per the current indications, the non-major ports will have an edge over the major ports due to their growth rates as a number of greenfield ports are coming up with huge capacities through the participation of the private sector in the non-major ports.

Table 1.6: Traffic Handled at the Minor and Intermediate Ports (Maritime State/UT-wise)

(In 1000 tonnes)

Year	*2010-2011*		*2011-2012*	
Name of the State	*Total*	*per cent*	*Total*	*per cent*
Gujarat	230907	73.34	259029	73.38
Maharashtra	14875	4.72	19948	5.65
Goa	14581	4.63	14470	4.10
Tamil Nadu	1611	0.51	1210	0.34
Karnataka	3095	0.98	687	0.19
Kerala	124	0.04	118	0.03
Puducherry (UT)	4712	1.50	6195	1.75
Andhra Pradesh	43269	13.74	45633	12.93
Orissa	320	0.10	4800	1.36
Andaman & Nicobar Islands (UT)	1354	0.43	925	0.26
Total	314848	100.00	353015	100.00

Source: Basic Port Statistics, MOST, GOI and Indian Ports Association (IPA) Report.

1.5 A Statewise Analysis of the Cargo Traffic

Gujarat is a principal maritime state endowed with a natural coastline of approximately 1,600 kms (about 29 per cent of India's total coastline). The state has 40 non-major ports. These have been under the administrative control of the Gujarat Maritime Board (GMB) since April 1982. Gujarat has the advantage of a vast hinterland covering the northern and the central Indian states and as a result, there is high demand for the services offered by the non-major ports in Gujarat. Further, through the Port Policy of 1995, the GMB has been securing the active participation of the private sector in the development of the non-major ports in Gujarat; there has been a steady increase in the infrastructure as well as growth in the volume of traffic being handled during the medium term. This traffic is handled mainly through 14 non-major ports. The remaining 26 are used for fishing activities and sailing-vessel traffic of small volume. The share of Gujarat in the total cargo handled by all the non-major ports in India has been increasing as a result of the successful development of the sector by the Gujarat Maritime Board.

Figure 1.3: Traffic Handled at Minor and Intermediate Ports: Maritime Statewise

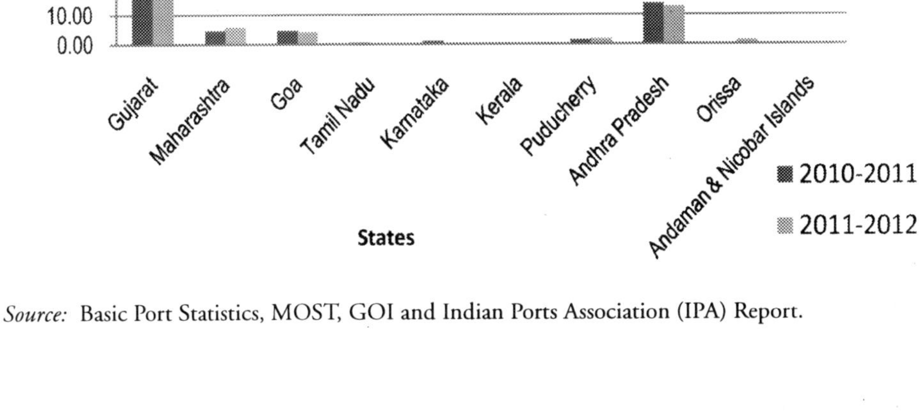

Source: Basic Port Statistics, MOST, GOI and Indian Ports Association (IPA) Report.

Table 1.7: Statewise Traffic being Handled at the Minor Ports (in million tonnes, 2009)

Year	*Gujarat*	*Maharashtra*	*Goa*	*Karnataka*	*Kerala*	*Tamil Nadu*	*Andhra Pradesh*	*Orissa*
1990-91	7.55	0.93	0.001	0.61	0.13	0.23	1.13	0.06
1991-92	8.9	0.53	0.01	0.38	0.13	0.19	1.18	0.15
1992-93	10.64	0.3	0.21	0.47	0.13	0.26	1.44	0.21
1993-94	13.09	0.65	0.21	0.31	0.1	0.08	1.81	0.21
1994-95	16.94	2.45	0.21	0.46	0.2	0.12	1.39	0.2
1995-96	17.15	3.65	0.06	0.35	-	0.11	2.31	0.17
1996-97	19.19	2.59	0.06	0.37	0.02	0.03	1.12	0.14
1997-98	26.84	4.68	0.37	0.52	0.2	0.27	1.77	0.2
1998-99	25.8	5.2	2.17	0.4	0.1	0.47	3.08	0.12
1999-00	48.8	5.91	2.02	0.48	0.1	0.41	3.81	0.15
2000-01	71.1	6.05	2.78	0.67	0.16	0.38	4.83	0.14
2001-02	82.55	4.98	2.9	0.68	0.13	0.53	3.51	0.02
2002-03	84.12	8.63	5.36	0.68	0.08	0.6	5.01	-
2003-04	89.35	10.33	8.44	1.17	0.05	0.69	10.02	-
2004-05	97.13	12.12	8.46	3.21	0.08	0.85	15.07	-
2005-06	103.2	11.11	11.86	2.44	0.08	0.71	15.09	-
2006-07	132.44	11.56	14.31	6.56	0.18	0.81	18.61	0.5

Source: Basic Port Statistics, MOST, GOI and Indian Ports Association (IPA) Report.

It is observed that of the maritime states, Gujarat comes first followed by Andhra Pradesh, Goa, Maharashtra, Karnataka, Tamil Nadu, Kerala and Orissa. In the global scenario, during the last decade, new technological developments have taken place especially in the port sector to accommodate container traffic. This has given rise to the demand of a new institutional set-up and major investment in this sector.

Gujarat stands second after Maharashtra (53) with a total of 40 Notified Minor ports. Out of these 40, only 19 are operational ports; others are merely "notified" where little or no cargo handling actually takes place. These ports have been identified by the respective governments to be developed in a phased manner; a good proportion of them involving a public–private partnership.

Figure 1.4: Minor Port Profile in India

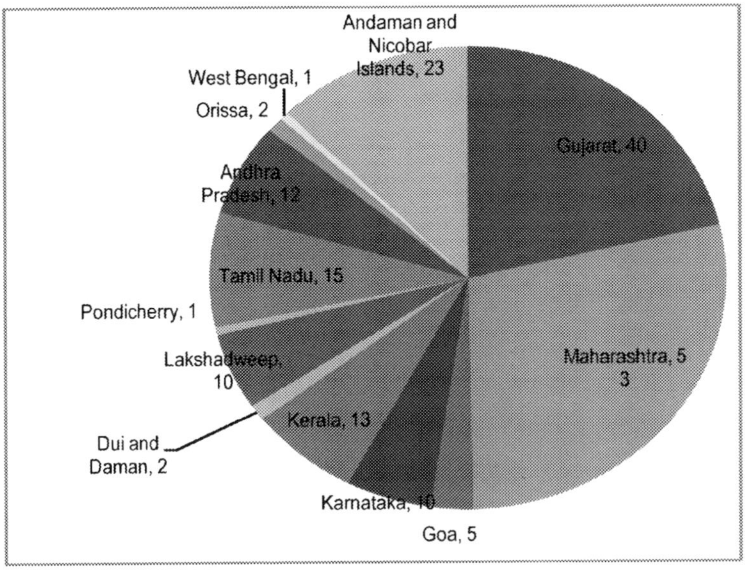

In order to encourage port-based industries, private companies have been granted permission to construct captive jetties for catering to their import–export requirement. As per this model, a port-based industry creates port facilities to import the industrial raw material and export the finished products. These captive jetties handle about 60 per cent of the total cargo at the GMB ports.

1.6 Commodity-Wise Traffic

In terms of the commodity-wise traffic at the 12 major ports, the increase during 2009–10 as compared to 2008–09 has been observed in all the broad categories of cargo except finished fertiliser and thermal coal. Amongst the dry bulk categories, fertiliser raw material (dry) and iron ore posted robust growth rates of 11.6 per cent and 6.7 per cent, respectively. Coking coal traffic, which is mainly imports, recorded a modest growth of 4.6 per cent. Container traffic, which largely reflects the trade in manufacturing goods and components, showed a significant growth of 8.7 per cent compared with a small increase of 1.02 per cent in 2008–09, while the other cargo traffic increased sharply by 20.9 per cent in 2009–10.

As expected, the maximum CAGR of 13.05 per cent has been noticed in container traffic, followed by 9.80 per cent for fertilizer and raw material and 8.18 per cent for the other miscellaneous cargo. The overall CAGR of the port traffic has been 7.28 per cent. It is pertinent to note that the last five years include the two years of 2008–09 and 2009–10 in which the growth of the port traffic was affected due to global slowdown and recession. If these two years are not considered and the previous three years i.e. 2005–06 to 2007–08 are taken into account, then the CAGR reached a level of 10.73 per cent.

As far as cargo composition is concerned, the pattern has remained unchanged during the past five years. During 2009–10, POL traffic maintained a predominant share of about 31 per cent, followed by container and iron ore traffic around 18 per cent, while the share of coal traffic was 13.8 per cent. This clearly shows that the investment made at the major ports in modern cargo-handling equipment has resulted in a growth of traffic over the years.

Table 1.8: Commodity-Wise Traffic Growth
(In million tonnes)

Commodity	*2005-06*	*2006-07*	*2007-08*	*2008-09*	*2009-10*	*CAGR during the last 5 years*	*CAGR during the last 3 years i.e. 2005-06 & 2007-08*
POL	142.09	154.34	168.75	176.14	175.08	5.36	8.98
Iron ore	79.17	80.59	91.80	94.04	100.33	6.10	7.68
Fertiliser	58.76	59.98	64.93	70.40	71.71	5.11	5.12
Coal	12.19	14.13	16.63	18.23	17.72	9.80	16.80
Container cargo	61.98	74.44	92.27	93.14	101.24	13.05	22.01
Other cargo	69.38	81.30	84.93	78.58	95.01	8.18	10.64
All Ports	423.57	464.78	519.31	530.53	561.09	7.28	10.73

Source: Basic Port Statistics, MOST, GOI and Indian Ports Association (IPA) Report.

In 2011–12, Petroleum Oil Lubricants/POL constituted the largest chunk of traffic at the Indian ports. With a minor decrease in its share, it may still continue to form the largest share in total traffic. Further, India is emerging as an important player for the export of refined products, which is expected to lead to a higher product movement. All these factors are seen as driving the POL traffic at the Indian ports over the next few years.

Figure 1.5: Share of Principal Commodities Handled at Major Ports during: 2011-12

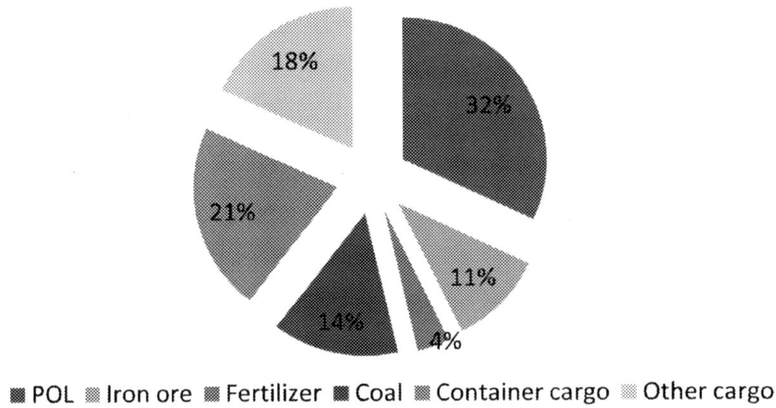

Source: Basic Port Statistics, MOST, GOI and Indian Ports Association (IPA) Report.

The domestic demand for steel is set to rise with many infrastructural initiatives being undertaken in the country. Consequently, the demand for coking coal may go up. On the other hand, the rise in capacities of the coal-based power utilities and cement plants is set to drive the demand for thermal coal. Coal-handling facilities at the operational non-major ports of Gangavaram, Krishnapatnam, Karaikal and the upcoming ports of Dighi, Dhamra and Gopalpur are expected to lead the increase in coal traffic at the non-major ports. With the rise in iron ore demand from the key ore-consuming countries like China, Korea and Japan, the Indian iron ore export is expected to continue to grow over the next few years.

The higher growth rate at the non-major ports can be attributed to the traffic that is increasingly being handled at the ports of Gangavaram and Krishnapatnam and the upcoming ports of Dhamra and Dighi.

India's trade basket towards manufacturers and containerisation increases its penetration of the general cargo traffic and the coal traffic is growing in order to meet the power sector and steel industry demands for the thermal and coking coal imports. The petroleum traffic also is expected to grow not only for India's domestic needs but also to support a growing petroleum products industry, with India beginning to emerge as a major refining centre for the region.

1.7 The Share of Major and Minor Ports in Cargo Traffic

The cargo handled by the minor ports in India was 38.66 per cent in the year 2011–12. In 2009–10, Gujarat's ports handled about 206 million tonnes of cargo, which accounted for 80 per cent of the cargo handled by all the minor ports of India. The major ports control two thirds (61.34 per cent) of the total cargo traffic handled in India. The share of the minor ports in cargo handling has grown briskly at over 30 per cent CAGR in the past, but there has been some decline in minor traffic in recent years. It is also noted that the share of the major ports has constantly declined and that of the minor ports has constantly increased. This is because of a gradual increase in the number of the minor ports.

Table 1.9: The Share of Major and Minor Ports

Years	*Major Ports*	*Minor Ports*	*Total*	*Per cent Share of Major Ports*	*Per cent Share of Minor Ports*	*Total*
1990-91	151.67	12.78	164.45	92.23	7.77	100.00
1991-92	156.64	13.26	169.90	92.27	7.63	100.00
1992-93	166.57	13.08	179.65	92.72	7.28	100.00
1993-94	179.26	14.23	193.49	92.65	7.35	100.00
1994-95	197.26	18.41	215.67	91.46	8.54	100.00
1995-96	215.34	24.16	239.50	89.91	10.09	100.00
1996-97	227.00	28.00	255.00	89.02	10.98	100.00
1997-98	251.49	34.78	286.27	87.85	12.15	100.00
1998-99	271.20	36.30	307.50	88.20	11.80	100.00
1999-00	272.00	63.00	335.00	81.19	18.81	100.00
2000-01	281.00	62.50	343.50	81.80	18.20	100.00
2001-02	287.70	80.00	367.70	78.24	21.76	100.00
2002-03	363.00	105.00	468.00	77.56	22.44	100.00
2003-04	390.00	128.62	518.62	75.20	24.70	100.00
2004-05	383.75	137.83	521.58	73.57	26.43	100.00
2005-06	423.57	155.22	578.79	73.18	26.82	100.00
2006-07	463.78	186.12	649.90	71.36	28.64	100.00
2007-08	519.31	203.48	722.79	71.85	28.15	100.00
2008-09	530.53	213.20	743.73	71.33	28.67	100.00
2009-10	561.09	288.80	849.89	66.02	33.98	100.00
2010-11	570.03	314.84	884.87	64.42	35.58	100.00
2011-12	560.13	353.02	913.15	61.34	38.66	100.00

Source: Basic Port Statistics, MOST, GOI and Indian Ports Association (IPA) Report.

The major ports and non-major ports in India collectively handled 913.15 million tonnes of cargo traffic during the year 2011–12 as compared to 884.87 million tonnes in 2010–11 and 849.89 million tonnes in 2009–10. Major ports account for over a 60 per cent share in 2011–12, which has come down since 1992-93 at the level of 92.72 per cent. Non-major ports unlike the major ports have improved their share and have strengthened their position in India's maritime trade. In 1990–91, the share of minor ports was just 7.77 per cent which gradually improved and reached up to 38.66 per cent within the very short span of twenty years.

Figure 1.6: Share of Major and Minor Ports (1990-91 to 2011-12)

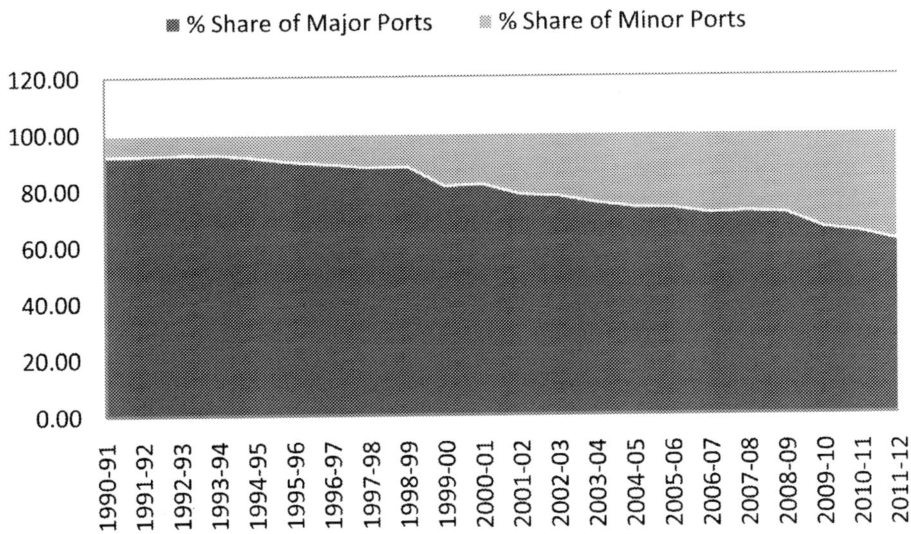

Source: Basic Port Statistics, MOST, GOI and Indian Ports Association (IPA) Report.

1.8 Capacity and Traffic at the Major Ports

In 1950, the traffic handled by the major ports was 19.2 MT, which grew to 560.15 MT in 2011–12; an almost 28 times increase in the last 60 years. The increase was maximum in the initial years because of a sharp increase in the cargo traffic. Till 1999–2000, the major ports had a lower capacity of traffic but after 2000 there has been a sharp increase. This clearly indicates the impact of port privatisation, corporatisation and the much-awaited response of globalisation which started in the early 1990s.

The Cargo traffic handling capacity of the major ports has been increasing over the years. The capacity which was placed at 169 million tonnes at the end of 1991–92 has increased to a level of around 616.73 million tonnes at the end of 2009–10 and 696.53 million tonnes at the end of 2011–12.

The capacity addition and the productivity improvements achieved by the major ports coupled with an increasing role of the non-major ports have changed the earlier scenario at the major ports wherein they were trying to cope with an excessive traffic to a situation where the ports, in general, wait for the ships. The capacity utilisation which was 92.6 per cent in 1991–92 and 97.3 per cent in 1992–93 was consistently above 100 until 1999–2000. The years 2000–01, 2001–02 and 2002–03 have witnessed a reversal of the trend with the capacity utilisation coming down to 96.46 per cent, 83.61 per cent and 86.44 per cent, respectively for all the major ports.[31] For the first time, the total cargo-handling capacity in the major ports exceeded the actual traffic handled in the year 2001 and the trend is still continuing. The capacity in the ports in 2010 was 616.73 million tonnes against the traffic of 561.09 million tonnes with a capacity utilisation of 90.98 per cent, which incidentally, is the lowest during the last five years. It shows that the capacity available was more than the traffic at the ports, which is an ideal situation.

Table 1.10: Major Ports: Capacity vis-à-vis Traffic (Traffic in MT)

Year	*Capacity*	*Traffic Handled*	*Difference*	*Per cent Capacity Utilisation*
1995-96	177.21	215.21	-38	121.44
1996-97	219.5	226.97	-7.47	103.40
1997-98	222	251.66	-29.66	113.36
1998-99	239.5	251.72	-12.22	105.10
1999-00	258.05	271.92	-13.87	105.37
2000-01	291.45	281.11	10.34	96.45
2001-02	344	287.59	56.41	83.60
2002-03	363	313.45	49.55	86.35
2003-04	390	344.799	45.201	88.41
2005-06	456.2	423.57	32.63	92.85
2006-07	504.75	463.78	40.97	91.88
2007-08	532.07	519.31	12.76	97.60
2008-09	574.77	530.53	44.24	92.30
2009-10	616.73	561.09	55.64	90.98
2011-12	696.53	560.15	136.38	80.42

Source: Basic Port Statistics, MOST, GOI and Indian Ports Association (IPA) Report.

Figure 1.7: Major Ports-Capacity vis-a-vis Traffic Handled (Traffic in MT)

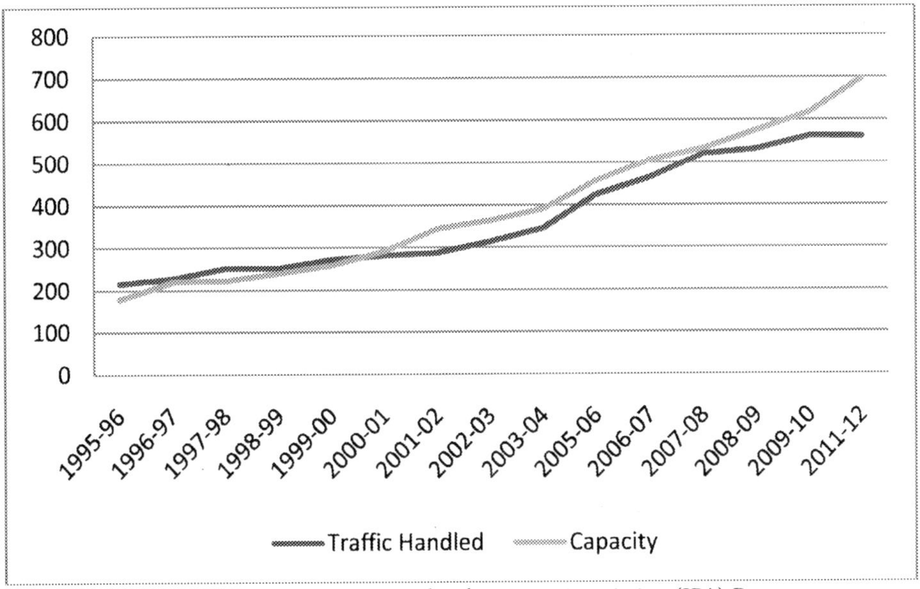

Source: Basic Port Statistics, MOST, GOI and Indian Ports Association (IPA) Report.

Adequate capacity is a good and healthier sign for the port sector. This will have a positive effect on cargo handling and port productivity. Capacity utilisation has varied between 80 to 97 per cent in the last ten years. Since 2000–2001, the aggregate capacity in the major ports has been in excess of the traffic handled. Consequently, capacity is no longer a constraint in the major ports. As a result, there has been a substantial improvement in their efficiency as borne out by the reduction in the waiting time for the ships. About 70 per cent of the cargo handled normally at these ports is for overseas trade, of which around 40 per cent constitutes exports. A number of initiatives have already been taken by the Ministry of Shipping and a rigorous monitoring is being done by the various wings of the Ministry for formulating and devising programmes for the enhancement of Port Capacity Projects. Private sector investment is being encouraged in the ports and several Public–Private Partnership projects have been envisaged for the enhancement of capacity.

NOTES

1 R. Ramakrishna, "Scenario of Port Handling and Vision", *Indian Ports*, Oct. 2003, pp.5-17.
2 http://en.wikipedia.org/wiki/Ports_in_India.
3 Animesh Ray, *Maritime India: Ports and Shipping*, Pearl Publishers, Kolkata, 1993.
4 Profile of Major Ports of India, May, 2005, IPA, New Delhi.
5 Basic Port Statistics of India, op.cit., 1.
6 Profile of Major Ports of India; Ibid.
7 http://en.wikipedia.org/wiki/Port_of_Kolkata.
8 Basic Port Statistics, MOST, GOI and Indian Ports Association (IPA) Report.
9 http://en.wikipedia.org/wiki/Paradip_Port.
10 Basic Port Statistics, MOST, GOI and Indian Ports Association (IPA) Report.
11 Basic Port Statistics, MOST, GOI and Indian Ports Association (IPA) Report.
12 http://www.vizagport.com.
13 http://en.wikipedia.org/wiki/Ennore_Port.
14 http://en.wikipedia.org/wiki/Tuticorin_Port_Trust.
15 Basic Port Statistics, MOST, GOI and Indian Ports Association (IPA) Report.
16 http://en.wikipedia.org/wiki/Cochin_Port.
17 http://www.newmangalore-port.com.
18 Basic Port Statistics, MOST, GOI and Indian Ports Association (IPA) Report.
19 http://en.wikipedia.org/wiki/Mormugao.
20 Basic Port Statistics, MOST, GOI and Indian Ports Association (IPA) Report.
21 http://en.wikipedia.org/wiki/Nhava_Sheva.
22 Basic Port Statistics, MOST, GOI and Indian Ports Association (IPA) Report.
23 http://jnport.gov.in/Performance.aspx?id=22&cid=18.
24 http://en.wikipedia.org/wiki/Mumbai_Port_Trust.
25 http://mumbaiport.gov.in.
26 http://mumbaiport.gov.in/index2.asp?slid=34&sublinkid=10&langid=1.
27 http://en.wikipedia.org/wiki/Kandla.
28 Ibid.
29 Ibid.
30 Basic Port Statistics, MOST, GOI and Indian Ports Association (IPA) Report.
31 Basic Port Statistics of India (2002-03), MOST, GOI, p.9.

2

Port Performance and Productivity

"Performance of a port depends on many factors which may be broadly divided into internal and external factors. External factors may be composed of trade orientation of the region in which the port is located, objectives of the local as well as central governments, and the geographical importance of the concerned location on the global map".[1] The purpose of this study is to highlight the role a port plays in India's regional economic development, and also to find the relationship between port performance, the demands of globalisation/liberalisation and the impact of corporatisation and privatisation. The importance of such work has increased since the initiation of the globalisation programme. No such research work exists which fully incorporates the impact of recent changes after globalisation on the port system in India, especially with reference to port performance and port productivity.

2.1. Introduction

The last six decades have experienced rapid changes in ocean transportation. Shipping has moved towards specialised vessels of larger size and higher speed.[2] These modern vessels are of high cost and therefore in order to increase the vessel utilisation[3] for the journey, there has been an increasing pressure to reduce the loading and unloading times at the seaports. The methods of cargo handling have therefore been modified from manual to automatic. In order to facilitate automatic handling, utilised packaging or containerisation has been gaining popularity. More than 60 per cent of the bulk cargo movement is in a containerised form today. Large container vessel capacity is around 10,000 Twenty Equivalent Units (TEUs) today, in place of less-than-1000 TEUs in the 1970s.

As the shipping demand increased, the demand for servicing them at the ports also increased, which has resulted in the development of a large number of new ports and the upgradation of existing ports.[4] Ports function as an interface between the land and the sea, providing facilities to handle the cargo to and from ships. Ships typically spend around 20 per cent of their time in ports. Any reduction in this time releases more time for the journey, which is revenue generating. Hence, the speed of service of the ships at the ports is very important.

2.2. A Model for Ranking the Major Ports

A model for ranking all the major ports has been developed for comparing, computing and understanding the changing position of the ports after the post-reform era, on the basis of operational performance indicators. Except the operational performance indicators, other indicators have also been identified and classified into separate categories—for example, financial performance indicators and the productivity of manpower and physical facilities-related indicators. The proposed model is shown in Figure 2.1.

Operational performance indicators have been used to establish an overall performance for each port for five points in time: 1991–92, 1996–97, 2003–04, 2008–09 and 2011–12. An interval of five years has been taken as criterion, but the years 2000–01 and 2001–02 were a turmoil years from the Indian maritime perspective because of cyclones on both the coasts. Therefore, it is justifiable to take the year 2003–04 for comparison and contrast. A composite index has been used to determine the performance of each port. This has been done for all the six operational performance indicators.

For obtaining the performance of the major ports, six important operational performance indicators have been selected. These indicators are Turn Around Time (in days), Pre-Berthing Detention Time (in days), Non-Working Time at Berth (in days). All are negative indicators of port performance on one side while on the other side positive indicators are Output per Ship Berthday (in tonnes), Cargo (in MT) by the port in a year and Number of Vessels Sailed by the ports in a year.

In order to make all the indicators unidirectional, negative indicators have been converted into positive indicators. A negative indicator means that a lower value represents a higher performance viz. Turn Around Time, Average Pre Berthing Detention and Non Working Time at Berth. Positive indicators imply that a higher value represents a higher efficiency or performance viz. Cargo Throughput, Output per Ship Berthday and the Number of Vessels Handled in year by the port.

2.3. An Analysis of Port Performance at the Major Ports (1991–2012)

The weighted score of each operational performance indicator has been calculated separately to find out a composite index, as is shown in Table 2.1. From the table it is comprehensible that the port of Ennore is operating with a maximum operational performance as well as productivity followed by the Jawaharlal Nehru Port. The most striking fact here is that both the ports are very recent in their origin as well as the fact that Ennore is the only corporatised port of India while the JNPT is in the process of corporatisation and it is expected that in the next few years it will be corporatised. So my basic assumption that corporatisation and privatisation enhance port performance is valid and also that it is the need of today's globalised era. Kandla and New Mangalore are placed at a third and fourth position, respectively. Here, it is worthwhile to mention that though the cargo-handling capacity of Kandla was maximum in 2011–12, its performance was not in the same sequence because of the other parameters of port performance viz. TRT, PBWT, NWTB, OSBD that have not performed up to the desired levels.

Figure 2.1: Performance Indicators of Major Ports in India

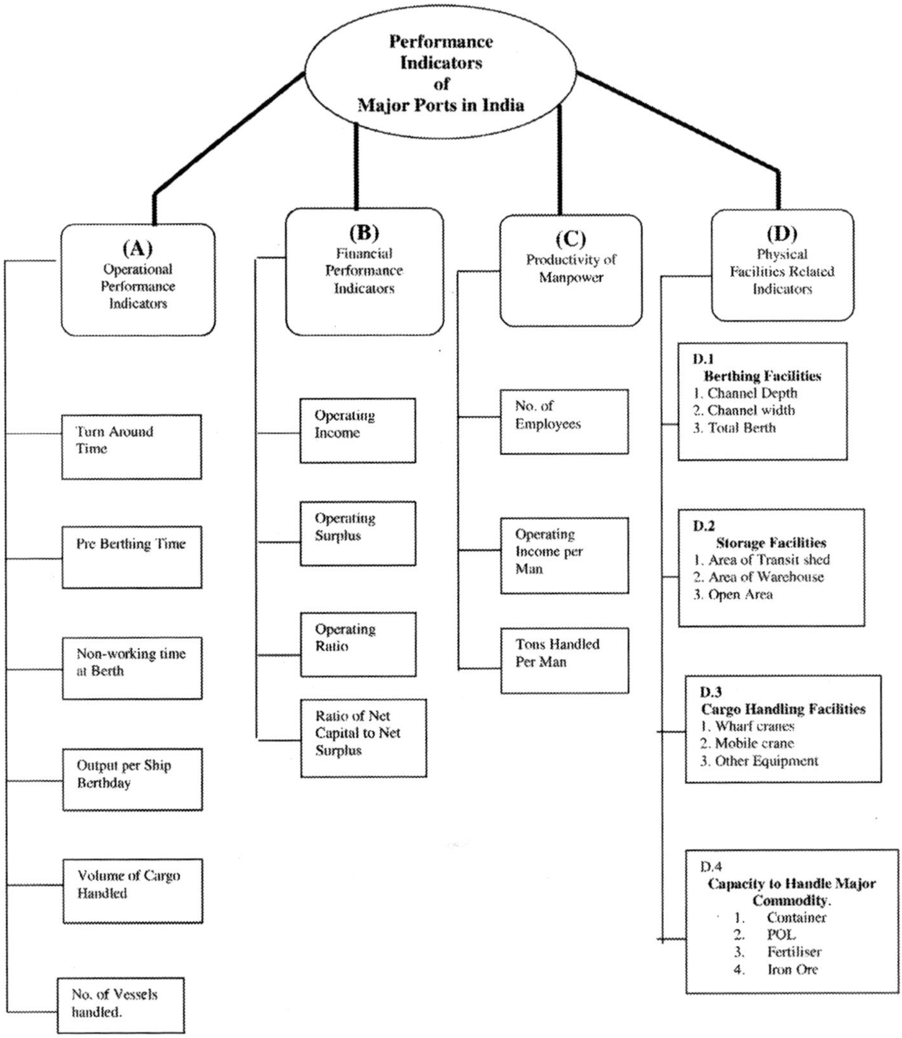

Source: Prepared on the basis of R. Sasikumar and Dr M. Bhasi, "A Comparative Study of Performance of India Major Sea Ports", Indian Ports, Vol 36 (2), Oct. 2004, p. 11.

Table 2.1: Performance of the Major Ports in India (1991–2012)

Name of the Major Port	*2011-12*		*2008-09*		*2003-04*		*1996-97*		*1991-92*	
	Value of C.I.	*Ranking*	*Value of C.I.*	*Ranking*	*Value of C.I.*	*Ranking*	*Value of C.I.*	*Ranking*	*Value of C.I.*	*Ranking*
Ennore	5.55	1	2.02	2	5.48	1				
JNPT	5.46	2	9.43	1	3.02	2	-0.37	6		
Visakhapatnam	-0.22	8	1.20	4	1.85	3	3.64	1	4.32	1
New Mangalore	1.19	4	0.17	6	1.64	4	0.18	4	-1.41	10
Kandla	1.63	3	1.85	3	0.95	5	-0.70	9	-0.64	8
Haldia	-2.52	10	-1.29	9	0.13	6	-1.13	10	0.27	7
Mumbai	0.96	5	-1.94	10	0.05	7	0.16	5	1.21	5
Cochin	0.82	6	-0.43	7	-0.49	8	1.96	2	3.30	2
Mormugao	-4.62	13	-3.01	12	-0.67	9	-2.89	12	2.70	3
Tuticorin	-3.38	11	-2.92	11	-1.86	10	-0.60	8	-0.91	9
Chennai	0.33	7	0.24	5	-1.91	11	-0.45	7	1.86	4
Paradip	-1.73	9	-1.29	8	-2.21	12	0.83	3	0.46	6
Kolkata	-3.47	12	-4.37	13	-5.56	13	-1.54	11	-4.20	11

Source: Ministry of Shipping, Road Transport & Highways, Govt. of India.

Newly incepted ports are performing better than the older existing ports. The performance of the newly developed ports is supported by a level of infrastructure, technological advancement, forward and backward linkages, etc. Since the inception of Ennore and JNPT, they have been performing reasonably well. The performance is because of a world-class infrastructure and a very high rate of containerisation at the port.

The performance of the Kolkata Port, as usual, is the poorest when compared with the other ports in India for almost all the selected years, followed by Mormugao, Tuticorin and Haldia from below. The maximum improved performance is noticed for the JNPT in the last ten years; the reason being that the JNPT is the only port of India which comprises an above 50 per cent mark of containerisation which has significantly reduced its Turn Around Time of ships and also to the Pre-Berthing Waiting Time for ships. The maximum downfall in performance is noticed for the port of Visakhapatnam, during 1991–2012. The Chennai Port has also noticed a remarkable decline because of the Ennore Port which started operation since 2001 and which is just 24 km north of the Chennai Port. Ennore has overtaken the role of the Chennai Port within two years of its functioning. In the same sequence, the second-most acute slide was experienced by the port of Paradip; here, Visakhapatnam has marginalised its importance because of containerisation and upgraded infrastructure. Ports like Tuticorin and Haldia have not recorded any significant changes in their position. The Ennore and JNPT ports are competing with each other for holding the premier position.

Satellite ports like Haldia, JNPT and Ennore have posed major challenges to their master ports of Kolkata, Mumbai and Chennai, respectively. The overall performance of the Mumbai Port is very poor due to the emergence of the JNPT which is nearby, with all the modern technological facilities and innovations. The port of Kolkata could survive because of the timely decision of the development of a new port, Haldia, which is more convenient to the customers. It has been noticed that slowly, the activities of the Kolkata port have come down and those for the Port of Haldia have gone up. Kolkata, Haldia and Kandla have the advantages of large port hinterlands where most of the industries are developed and where a good part of the agricultural products is produced.

One very interesting phenomena in the history of port performance is that the modern ports have always performed well in the initial years of their setup, like the port of Cochin performed very well after its inception and at a time (1991–92), ranked second; the JNPT which minimises the load of the Mumbai Port has worked as a responsible port since the date of its operation. In the same way, the Ennore Port has performed well over the years and today it is the premier port in terms of operational performance and efficiency. Changes in the performance recorded by the other ports are summarised in Table 2.1.

Table 2.2: Performance of the Major Ports in India (2011–12)

Name of the Major Port	*TRT (Days)*	*PBWT (Days)*	*NWTB (Days)*	*OSBD (Tonnes)*	*Cargo Handled in MT*	*No. of Vessels*	*Total Value*	*Ranking*
	X-Mean/ S.D.	*X-Mean/ S.D.*	*X-Mean/ S.D.*	*X-Mean/ S.D.*	*X-Mean/ S.D.*	*X-Mean/ S.D.*	*X-Mean/ S.D.*	
Kolkata	-0.78	1.49	-0.72	-1.57	-1.45	-0.44	-3.47	12
Haldia	-0.12	-0.87	-0.58	-0.90	-0.57	0.51	-2.52	10
Visakhapatnam	-0.83	-0.98	-0.40	-0.26	1.14	1.11	-0.22	8
Chennai	-0.26	0.35	-0.64	-0.32	0.59	0.62	0.33	7
Tuticorin	-0.64	-0.53	-0.53	-0.90	-0.70	-0.08	-3.38	11
Cochin	1.82	0.59	0.22	0.54	-1.08	-1.26	0.82	6
New Mangalore	0.33	1.40	0.22	0.25	-0.48	-0.53	1.19	4
Mumbai	1.58	0.01	-0.33	-0.94	0.62	0.03	0.96	5
JNPT	0.81	0.41	0.40	1.09	1.07	1.69	5.46	2
Kandla	-0.98	-1.20	0.18	0.30	1.85	1.46	1.63	3
Paradip	-0.96	-1.19	-0.39	0.58	0.52	-0.29	-1.73	9
Mormugao	-1.16	-1.01	-0.63	-0.29	-0.19	-1.33	-4.62	13
Ennore	1.19	1.53	3.22	2.41	-1.32	-1.48	5.55	1

Source: Ministry of Shipping, Road Transport & Highways, Govt. of India.

Table 2.2 depicts that the Ennore Port is ranked first in terms of the cumulative parameters followed by the JNPT and Kandla. Mormugao and Tuticorin are the worst performers amongst all the major ports.

Table 2.3: Performance of the Major Ports in India (2008–09)

Name of the Major Port	*TRT (Days)*	*PBWT (Days)*	*NWTB (Days)*	*OSBD (Tonnes)*	*Cargo Handled in MT*	*No. of Vessels*	*Total Value*	*Ranking*
	X-Mean/ S.D.	*X-Mean/ S.D.*	*X-Mean/ S.D.*	*X-Mean/ S.D.*	*X-Mean/ S.D.*	*X-Mean/ S.D.*	*X-Mean/ S.D.*	
Kolkata	-0.75	0.22	-0.63	-1.30	-1.46	-0.46	-4.37	13
Haldia	-0.57	-0.40	-0.40	-0.57	0.05	0.60	-1.29	9
Visakhapatnam	-0.41	-0.15	-0.25	-0.05	1.19	0.89	1.20	4
Chennai	-0.54	-0.19	-0.39	-0.11	0.86	0.61	0.24	5
Tuticorin	-0.24	-0.08	-0.45	-0.87	-0.97	-0.31	-2.92	11
Cochin	1.52	0.18	-0.18	-0.14	-1.32	-0.50	-0.43	7
New Mangalore	0.30	0.24	0.07	0.33	-0.21	-0.56	0.17	6
Mumbai	-0.81	-0.19	-0.59	-0.88	0.57	-0.03	-1.94	10
JNPT	2.06	-0.01	3.38	1.36	0.85	1.81	9.43	1
Kandla	-0.98	-0.36	-0.10	0.25	1.62	1.43	1.85	3
Paradip	-0.83	-0.33	-0.36	0.18	0.29	-0.24	-1.29	8
Mormugao	-0.21	-0.27	-0.28	-0.80	0.04	-1.51	-3.01	12
Ennore	1.14	1.35	0.16	2.60	-1.51	-1.73	2.02	2

Source: Ministry of Shipping, Road Transport & Highways, Govt. of India.

Table 2.4: Performance Indicators of the Major Ports (2003–04)

Ports	*TRT (Days)*	*PBWT (Days)*	*NWTB (Days)*	*OSBD (Tonnes)*	*Cargo (MT)*	*No. of Vessels Sailed*
Kolkata	4.29	0.51	1.14	3384	8.69	765
Haldia	2.84	0.97	0.73	8280	32.57	1889
Visakhapatnam	3.33	0.76	0.59	11712	47.74	1704
Chennai	4.85	2.28	1.03	9517	36.71	1656
Tuticorin	2.52	0.70	0.76	5084	13.68	1517
Cochin	2.22	0.43	0.59	7799	13.57	1133
New Mangalore	2.35	0.55	0.53	17955	26.67	879
Mumbai	4.07	0.87	0.47	5911	29.92	1800
JNPT	1.85	0.76	1.23	9845	31.27	3681
Kandla	5.06	2.03	0.45	8659	41.52	1823
Paradip	3.43	0.53	0.99	10257	25.31	1041
Mormugao	4.47	2.60	0.50	16746	27.87	677
Ennore	2.11	0.07	0.49	32777	9.28	166
All Ports	3.45	1.10	0.73	9079	344.80	18731

Source: Compiled from Basic Port Statistics of India, MOST, GOI and Indian Infrastructure, March 2005.

Table 2.5: Composite Indices of the Major Ports (2003–04)

Ports	*C.I. 1*	*C.I. 2*	*C.I. 3*	*C.I. 4*	*C.I. 5*	*C.I. 6*	*Composite Index*
	TRT (Days)	*PBWT (Days)*	*NWTB (Days)*	*OSBD (Tonnes)*	*Cargoin MT*	*No. of Vessels Sailed*	
Kolkata	-0.88	-0.09	-1.30	-1.05	-1.46	-0.79	-5.56
Haldia	0.20	-0.35	-0.33	-0.41	0.49	0.52	0.13
Visakhapatnam	-0.27	-0.27	0.30	0.04	1.73	0.31	1.85
Chennai	-1.13	-0.51	-1.12	-0.24	0.83	0.25	-1.91
Tuticorin	0.61	-0.24	-0.44	-0.82	-1.05	0.09	-1.86
Cochin	1.10	0.00	0.30	-0.47	-1.06	-0.36	-0.49
New Mangalore	0.87	-0.13	0.68	0.86	0.01	-0.65	1.64
Mumbai	-0.77	-0.32	1.15	-0.72	0.28	0.42	0.05
JNPT	1.91	-0.27	-1.43	-0.20	0.39	2.61	3.02
Kandla	-1.20	-0.50	1.34	-0.36	1.22	0.44	0.95
Paradip	-0.35	-0.11	-1.04	-0.15	-0.10	-0.47	-2.21
Mormugao	-0.97	-0.52	0.90	0.70	0.11	-0.89	-0.67
Ennore	1.31	3.28	0.98	2.80	-1.41	-1.48	5.48

Source: Compiled from Basic Port Statistics of India, MOST, GOI and Indian Infrastructure, March 2005.

Table 2.6: Summary of the Major Port Performance

Ports	*Year*	*Better Performing Years*
Kolkata	1870	Initially conceived to promote and protect the British colonial interests. But with the advent of freedom in 1947, the port was called upon to play the opposite; to champion the national cause and was rightly called as "gateway to Eastern India". Its performing efficiency has reduced because of old infrastructure, low manpower productivity and a high cost of cargo handling.
Mumbai	1873	It is known as the "Gateway of Modern India" or "the Nation's Window to the Outside World" solely because of its performance for several decades, but its role has taken over by the JNPT.
Chennai	1881	Performed well in 1991–92 with rank four after Visakhapatnam, Cochin and Mormugao.
Cochin	1930	Performed exceptionally well in the 1990s, with having a second position since 1991–92 to 1996–97.
Visakhapatnam	1933	Constantly performed its best in the years 1991–92 to 1996–97, with a first rank.
Kandla	1955	Best performance was in 1985–86 and it ranked first; also performed better in 2003–04, 2008–09 and 2011–12.

Ports	*Year*	*Better Performing Years*
Mormugao	1963	Performed very well in 1991–92 and reached the third position. The port today accounts for about 50 per cent of India's iron ore export and ranks within the first ten leading iron ore exporting ports of the world.
Paradip	1965	The better performing years for the port were from 1991–92 to 1996–97.
New Mangalore	1975	Improving its position since inception and in 2003–04, ranked fourth.
Haldia	1977	Performed well in the 1980s and ranked third in 1985–86.
Tuticorin	1979	Never achieved any significant position; only in the initial years had performed better.
JNPT	1989	Better years or performance after 1996–97, when containerisation had rapidly taken place and also performed its best sometime during 2000–2002[5] and 2008–09.
Ennore	2001	Its best performance was in the years 2003–04 and 2011–12.

Source: Based on Ghosh and De[6] and the data used for this study.

Table 2.7: Performance Indicators of the Major Ports (1996–97)

Ports	*TRT (Days)*	*PBWT (Days)*	*NWTB (Days)*	*OSBD (Tonnes)*	*Cargo (in MT)*	*No. of Vessels Sailed*
Kolkata	7.7	0.95	2.66	1188	6.02	874
Haldia	6	2.19	1.55	5855	17.1	947
Visakhapatnam	5.66	1.6	0.83	6696	34.5	1437
Chennai	7.8	4.07	1.82	5131	31.85	1681
Tuticorin	5.16	1.56	1.48	3026	9.18	905
Cochin	3.9	1.12	1.26	5438	11.74	784
New Mangalore	4.43	1.51	1.35	7172	12.45	644
Mumbai	10.67	4.57	2.21	2605	33.73	2616
JNPT	6.3	2.14	0.71	2987	8.07	640
Kandla	10.56	6.61	1.18	7066	33.73	1527
Paradip	4.9	1.61	0.8	6406	11.58	557
Mormugao	6.3	2.2	3.03	8540	17.31	507
All Ports	7.5	3.1	1.45	4497	227.26	13119

Source: Compiled from Basic Port Statistics of India (1996 and 1997), MOST, GOI.

In 1996–97, the best performance was by the port of Visakhapatnam, followed by Cochin and Paradip. The poorest performance was by Mormugao, Kolkata and Haldia respectively. The JNPT has improved its position by building its infrastructure to international standards with a high level of automation and computerised functioning while no improvement has been noticed for the Kolkata port because of old infrastructure which is also deteriorating day by day. One major change which comes out of the computation is that the JNPT has improved its efficiency through Privatisation, Corporatisation and Containerisation but the importance of the Mumbai Port has reduced. One very important factor for the low performance of the Indian ports is that their financial position is not good for future growth and development, except for the ports of JNPT, Ennore and Chennai. This is mainly due to the high expenditure incurred by the ports. Besides these, the real culprit is the non-productive expenditure, which has to be contained in the case of Cochin and Mumbai.

Another reason for the low performance of the Indian ports is that all the old ports have higher staff strength because, the port sector was considered as an important employment sector after Independence. Now the situation has changed and a port like the JNPT has least manpower followed by New Mangalore and Tuticorin. So, the latest developed ports have less staff strength due to a change in the technology of the material handling system. Old ports are now changing the technology towards automation. So, it is very difficult to reduce their staff strength all of a sudden due to a resistance from all corners.

Table 2.8: Composite Indices of the Major Ports (1996–97)

Ports	*C.I. 1 TRT (Days)*	*C.I. 2 PBWT (Days)*	*C.I. 3 NWTB (Days)*	*C.I. 4 OSBD (Tonnes)*	*C.I. 5 Cargo in MT*	*C.I. 6 No. of Vessels Sailed*	*Composite Index*
Kolkata	-0.80	1.90	-1.13	-1.78	-1.15	-0.35	-1.54
Haldia	-0.07	-0.31	-0.36	0.30	-0.16	-0.24	-1.13
Visakhapatnam	0.13	0.31	1.24	0.68	1.39	0.56	3.64
Chennai	-0.84	-1.09	-0.63	-0.02	1.15	0.95	-0.45
Tuticorin	0.48	0.37	-0.27	-0.96	-0.87	-0.30	-0.60
Cochin	1.73	1.31	0.07	0.12	-0.64	-0.50	1.96

Ports	*C.I. 1 TRT (Days)*	*C.I. 2 PBWT (Days)*	*C.I. 3 NWTB (Days)*	*C.I. 4 OSBD (Tonnes)*	*C.I. 5 Cargo in MT*	*C.I. 6 No. of Vessels Sailed*	*Composite Index*
New Mangalore	1.11	0.45	-0.08	0.89	-0.58	-0.73	0.18
Mumbai	-1.53	-1.19	-0.91	-1.15	1.32	2.46	0.16
JNPT	-0.23	-0.27	1.82	-0.98	-0.97	-0.73	-0.37
Kandla	-1.51	-1.44	0.22	0.84	1.32	0.70	-0.70
Paradip	0.68	0.30	1.37	0.55	-0.66	-0.87	0.83
Mormugao	-0.23	-0.32	-1.26	1.50	-0.15	-0.95	-2.89

Source: Compiled from Basic Port Statistics of India (1996 and 1997), MOST, GOI.

To overcome the above-mentioned problems, proper planning, developmental schemes and a well-designed implementation schedule must be evolved for the success of the Major Ports in India. At the same time, the old ports have to restructure their infrastructural facilities as well as add new technological inputs.

Table 2.9: Performance Indicators of the Major Ports (1991–92)

Ports	*TRT (Days)*	*PBWT (Days)*	*NWTB (Days)*	*OSBD (Tonnes)*	*Cargo in MT*	*No. of Vessel Sailed*
Kolkata	10.52	0.75	3.44	612	4.00	717
Haldia	5.96	1.52	1.62	5861	12.00	703
Visakhapatnam	5.58	1.02	1.23	6120	21.52	928
Chennai	5.98	1.56	2.14	4579	25.05	1381
Tuticorin	5.19	1.26	1.65	2196	5.87	724
Cochin	3.95	0.79	1.44	4124	7.48	621
New Mangalore	5.5	1.67	1.83	4564	8.27	452
Mumbai	7.48	1.55	3.05	2825	26.26	2106
Kandla	8.59	3.56	1.61	5322	21.00	1022
Paradip	6.08	1.17	1.15	4919	7.30	347
Mormugao	5.96	0.87	2.42	10343	15.10	601
All Ports	6.65	1.54	2.13	20584	153.85	1970

Source: Compiled from Basic Port Statistics of India (1991 and 1992), MOST, GOI.

Table 2.10: Composite Indices of the Major Ports (1991–92)

Ports	*C1 TRT (Days)*	*C2 PBWT (Days)*	*C3 NWTB (Days)*	*C4 OSBD (Tonnes)*	*C5 Cargo in MT*	*C6 No. of Vessels Sailed*	*Composite Index*
Kolkata	-1.62	1.70	-1.31	-1.55	-1.16	-0.25	-4.20
Haldia	0.19	-0.41	0.41	0.55	-0.18	-0.28	0.27
Visakhapatnam	0.48	0.59	1.44	0.65	0.98	0.17	4.32
Chennai	0.18	-0.47	-0.38	0.03	1.41	1.09	1.86
Tuticorin	0.82	0.01	0.35	-0.92	-0.93	-0.24	-0.91
Cochin	2.33	1.49	0.81	-0.15	-0.74	-0.44	3.30
New Mangalore	0.55	-0.60	0.03	0.03	-0.64	-0.78	-1.41
Mumbai	-0.66	-0.45	-1.12	-0.67	1.56	2.54	1.21
Kandla	-1.09	-1.59	0.43	0.33	0.92	0.36	-0.64
Paradip	0.11	0.20	1.73	0.17	-0.76	-1.00	0.46
Mormugao	0.19	1.12	-0.67	2.34	0.20	-0.48	2.70

Source: Compiled from Basic Port Statistics of India (1991 and 1993), MOST, GOI.

Table 2.11: Comparative Performance of the Major Ports in the Post-Reform Era

Improved	*Static but Poor*	*Declined*
Ennore	Haldia	Kolkata
JNPT	Tuticorin	Cochin
New Mangalore		Chennai
Kandla		Paradip
		Mormugao
		Mumbai
		Visakhapatnam

Source: Compiled on the basis of Table 2.1 to 2.10.

At the beginning of the post-reform era, Visakhapatnam was operating with a maximum operational performance and productivity followed by Cochin. Mormugao and Chennai had the third and fourth positions, respectively. The operational performance of the port of Kolkata was the poorest when compared with the other ports in India, which was followed by New Mangalore (second poorest performer).

2.4 Turn Around Time at the Major Ports of India (1991–2012)

There has been general reduction in the average Turn Around Time (TRT) at all the major ports in the country during the last 20 years. The average TRT was 6.7 days in 1991–92 at all the ports. The TRT days have significantly declined over the years to reach a level of 4.56 days in 2011–12. The ports which have shown a considerable improvement in TRT include the JNPT followed by the Ennore and Cochin ports. The maximum TRT is observed for the ports of Mumbai, Kandla, Kolkata, Chennai and Mormugao. The average TRT is influenced by a number of factors like the type of cargo, parcel size, PBD, entrance channel, containerisation, modernisation of port infrastructure, etc. In 2011–12, the TRT has been the least in the case of the container vessels.

Table 2.12: Turn Around Time at the Major Ports of India (1991–2012)

Name of the Major Port	*TRT (in Days)*				
	2011-12	*2008-09*	*2003-04*	*1996-97*	*1991-92*
Kolkata	5.45	4.60	4.29	7.7	10.52
Haldia	3.62	4.21	2.84	6	5.96
Visakhapatnam	5.68	3.93	3.33	5.66	5.58
Chennai	3.91	4.15	4.85	7.8	5.98
Tuticorin	4.94	3.66	2.52	5.16	5.19
Cochin	1.82	2.14	2.22	3.9	3.95
New Mangalore	2.95	3.00	2.35	4.43	5.5
Mumbai	1.94	4.73	4.07	10.67	7.48
Kandla	6.42	5.2	5.06	10.56	8.59
Paradip	6.33	4.78	3.43	4.9	6.08
Mormugao	7.68	3.61	4.47	6.3	5.96
JNPT	2.46	1.9	1.85	6.3	
Ennore	2.17	2.35	2.11		

Source: Ministry of Shipping, Road Transport & Highways, Govt. of India.

Fig. 2.2: Turn Around Time at Major Ports of India (1991-2012)

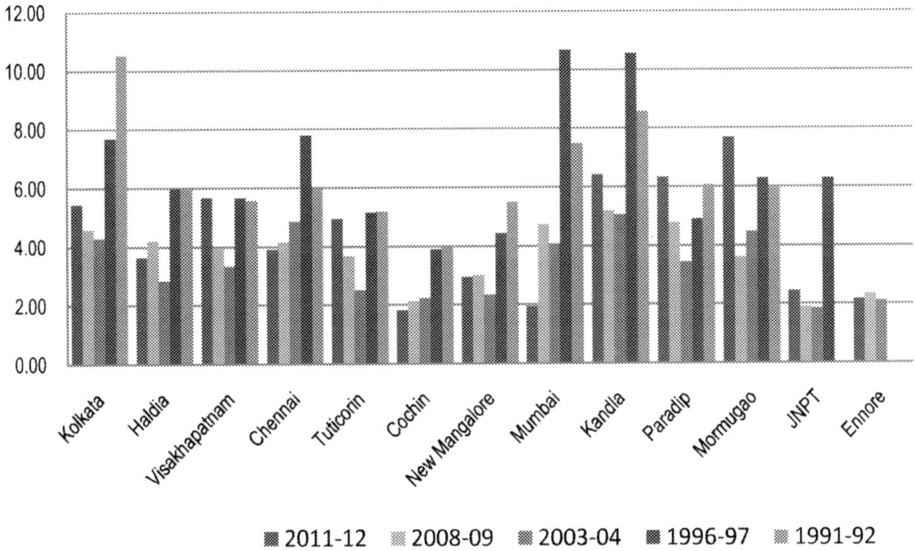

Source: Ministry of Shipping, Road Transport & Highways, Govt. of India.

At the individual port level, the ports which recorded an average TRT higher than all the other ports (an average of 3.45 days in 2003–04) were Kolkata, Chennai, Mumbai, Kandla and Mormugao. The lowest was in the case of the JNPT followed by the port of Ennore. The average TRT, except in respect of the ports at Tuticorin, New Mangalore, Kandla and Mumbai, showed an improvement in 2011–12. At the port level, ports at Kolkata, Paradip, Visakhapatnam, Tuticorin, Mormugao, Mumbai and Kandla recorded a TRT which was more than the average for all the major ports at 4.56 days. The minimum was at Cochin (1.82 days) and the maximum (7.68 days) at Mormugao.

2.5 Average Pre-Berthing Detention Time (PBDT)

The average overall Pre-berthing Detention Time (PBDT) for all the major ports declined from 2.2 days in 1990–91 to 0.96 days in 2004–05. Thereafter, the average PBDT for all the major ports has shown an increase to 1.63 days in 2008–09 and 2.32 days in 2010–11. However, the average PBDT on port account has seen a sharper decline from 2.10 days in 1990–

91 to 0.2 days in 2004–05. In 2012–13, the average PBDT on port account increased to 0.45 days.

Table 2.13: Pre-Berthing Waiting Time at the Major Ports of India (1991–2012)

Name of the Major Port	*PBWT (in Days)*				
	2011-12	*2008-09*	*2003-04*	*1996-97*	*1991-92*
Kolkata	0.77	0.66	0.51	0.95	0.75
Haldia	2.54	3.38	0.97	2.19	1.52
Visakhapatnam	2.84	1.28	0.76	1.6	1.02
Chennai	1.16	1.39	2.28	4.07	1.56
Tuticorin	1.91	1.09	0.7	1.56	1.26
Cochin	1.05	0.70	0.43	1.12	0.79
New Mangalore	0.79	0.65	0.55	1.51	1.67
Mumbai	1.37	1.41	0.87	4.57	1.55
Kandla	3.74	2.62	2.03	6.61	3.56
Paradip	3.69	2.32	0.53	1.61	1.17
Mormugao	2.94	1.77	2.6	2.2	0.87
JNPT	1.13	0.95	0.76	2.14	
Ennore	0.76	0.27	0.07		

Source: Ministry of Shipping, Road Transport & Highways, Govt. of India.

The position in respect of the average Pre-Berthing Detention Time (PBDT) at all the major ports during 1991–92 to 2011–12 is brought out in Fig. 2.3. The average PBDT of the vessels which rose in the first half of the 1990s from 1.6 days in 1991–92 touched a high of 3.6 days in 1995–96. This has been reversed since then with a steady decline to 1 day in 2004–05. However, from 2005–06 onwards, the average PBDT started to increase. In 2010–11, the average PBDT of the vessels increased to 2.32 days compared to 2.16 days in 2009–10. The average PBDT of the vessels declined to 2.05 days in 2011–12. During 2011–12, the ports at Kolkata, Haldia, Chennai, Mormugao, Paradip and JNPT experienced a drop in the pre-berthing detention of vessels.

The average PBDT depends on a variety of factors attributable to port account and non-port account. The decrease in the PBDT in 2011–12 to 2.05 days as compared to 2.32 days in 2010–11 was due to a combination of both the port and non-port factors. The PBDT on non-port account decreased from 1.82 days in 2010–11 to 1.60 days in 2011–12 whereas on port account it decreased by 0.05 days. The data on the PBDT for the different types of vessels indicates that in 2011–12, the average PBDT was the least (0.77 days) in the case of container vessels followed by liquid bulk vessels (1.74 days), break bulk (2.66 days), dry bulk (3.52 days) and dry bulk (4.12 days).

All the ports recorded a decrease in the PWDT in 2003–04; the lowest PBD time was for the port of Ennore followed by Cochin. The average PBDT depends on a multiplicity of factors attributable to port account and non-port account. The marginal increase in PBDT in 2001–02 to 1.4 days, as compared to 1.2 days in 2000–01 could be attributed mainly to reasons pertaining to non-port account.

Fig. 2.3: Pre-Berthing Waiting Time at Major Ports of India (1991-2012)

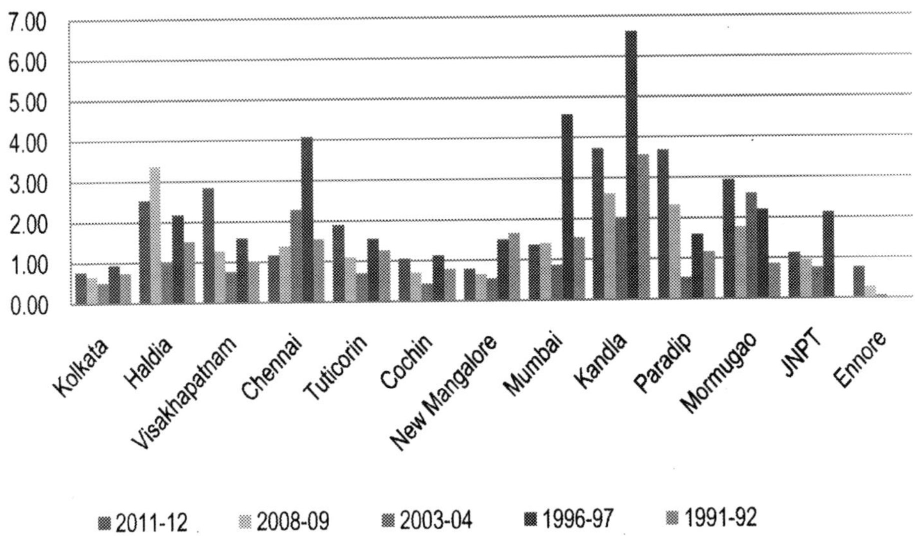

Source: Ministry of Shipping, Road Transport & Highways, Govt. of India.

The highest PBDT at the major ports of India during 1991–2012 was recorded for ports of Kandla, Mumbai, Chennai, Paradip, Haldia and Mormugao. Kandla, Mumbai and Chennai ports have handled a significant percentage of the cargo. In addition, these ports cover very a large hinterland for the purpose of import and export. Therefore, for these ports, it is obvious that the total number of the incoming and outgoing vessels would be greater than any other port, which leads to a higher PBWT. Moreover, these ports handle general cargo only and they do not have any specialisation in the handling of commodities.

Table 2.14: Non-Working Time at Berth by the Major Ports of India (1991–2012)

Name of the Major Port	*NWBT (in Days)*				
	2011-12	*2008-09*	*2003-04*	*1996-97*	*1991-92*
Kolkata	1.16	1.08	1.14	2.66	3.44
Haldia	0.84	0.66	0.73	1.55	1.62
Visakhapatnam	0.63	0.53	0.59	0.83	1.23
Chennai	0.96	0.65	1.03	1.82	2.14
Tuticorin	0.77	0.72	0.76	1.48	1.65
Cochin	0.33	0.48	0.59	1.26	1.44
New Mangalore	0.33	0.37	0.53	1.35	1.83
Mumbai	0.57	0.97	0.47	2.21	3.05
Kandla	0.34	0.44	0.99	0.8	1.15
Paradip	0.95	0.62	0.5	3.03	2.42
Mormugao	0.62	0.55	0.45	1.18	
JNPT	0.29	0.09	1.23	0.71	1.61
Ennore	0.10	0.34	0.49		

Source: Ministry of Shipping, Road Transport & Highways, Govt. of India.

All the three negative indicators viz. TRT, PBDT and NWTB together determine the performance and efficiency of port functioning. Higher the value of negative indicator, lower the performance, whereas lower the value, higher the performance. There has been a general decline in the NWTB for all the major ports of India during 1991–2012. The least NWTB was recorded for the ports of Ennore, JNPT, Cochin, New Mangalore and Kandla. The reason for a poor performance by the ports of Kolkata, Chennai, Paradip and Haldia is owing to a high NWTB (which means a lower productivity of the NWTB).

Fig. 2.4: Non-Working Time at Berth - Major Ports of India (1991-2012)

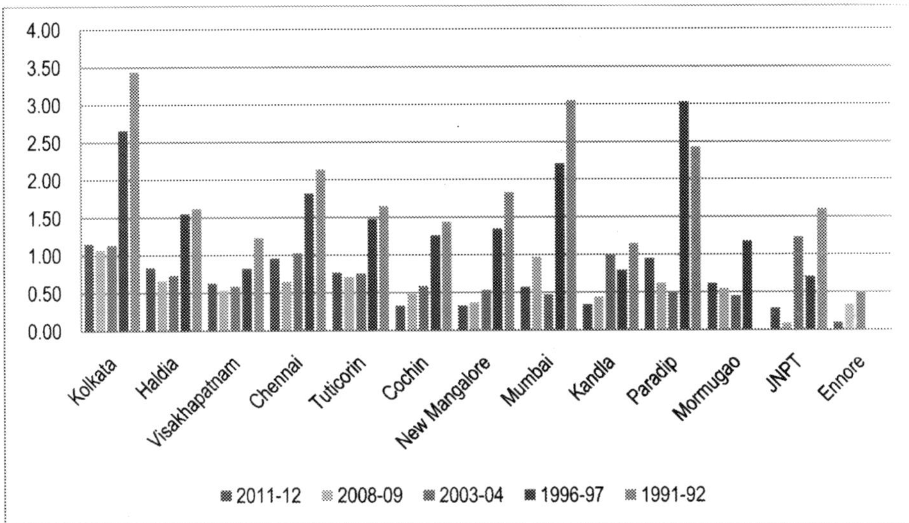

Source: Ministry of Shipping, Road Transport & Highways, Govt. of India.

There has been a gradual decrease in the NWTB. In 1991–92, it was 2.13 days which decreased to 1.45 days in 1996–97 and in 2003–04 reached to the level of 0.73 days. Though a decrease has been noticed over a period of time, if we compare it to the international levels, then India is far behind the port of Singapore and the port of Rotterdam where there is no concept of NWTB as well as a PBDT for the ports.

2.6 The Average Output per Ship Berthday

The average output per ship berthday has become almost three times, from 3942 tonnes in 1991–92 to 10575 tonnes in 2011–12. The ports at Kolkata, Paradip, Ennore, Cochin, Mormugao, Mumbai and Kandla have shown an improvement in the output per ship berthday in 2011–12. An important determinant of the output per ship berthday during 2011–12 was seen in the case of the Ennore Port followed by the JNPT. New Mangalore, Paradip, Chennai and Visakhapatnam are major ports with the major quantities of dry bulk cargo being handled by mechanical means and therefore they have had a higher output per ship berthday.

Table 2.15: Output per Ship Berthday at Major Ports of India (1991–2012) (in Tonnes)

Name of the Major Port	*Output per Ship Berthday (in Tonnes)*				
	2011-12	*2008-09*	*2003-04*	*1996-97*	*1991-92*
Kolkata	2503.00	3027.00	3384	1188	612
Haldia	6728.00	7732.00	8280	5855	5861
Visakhapatanam	10704.00	11171.00	11712	6696	6120
Chennai	10352.00	10778.00	9517	5131	4579
Tuticorin	6733.00	5817.00	5084	3026	2196
Cochin	15784.00	10599.00	7799	5438	4124
New Mangalore	13957.00	13645.00	17955	7172	4564
Mumbai	6476.00	5717.00	5911	2605	2825
Kandla	14272.00	13107.00	8659	7066	5322
Paradip	15995.00	12635.00	10257	6406	4919
Mormugao	10530.00	6290.00	16746	8540	10343
JNPT	19227.00	20344.00	9845	2987	
Ennore	27505.00	28424.00	32777		

Source: Ministry of Shipping, Road Transport & Highways, Govt. of India.

Fig. 2.5: Output Per Ship Berthday at Major Ports of India (1991-2012) (in Tonnes)

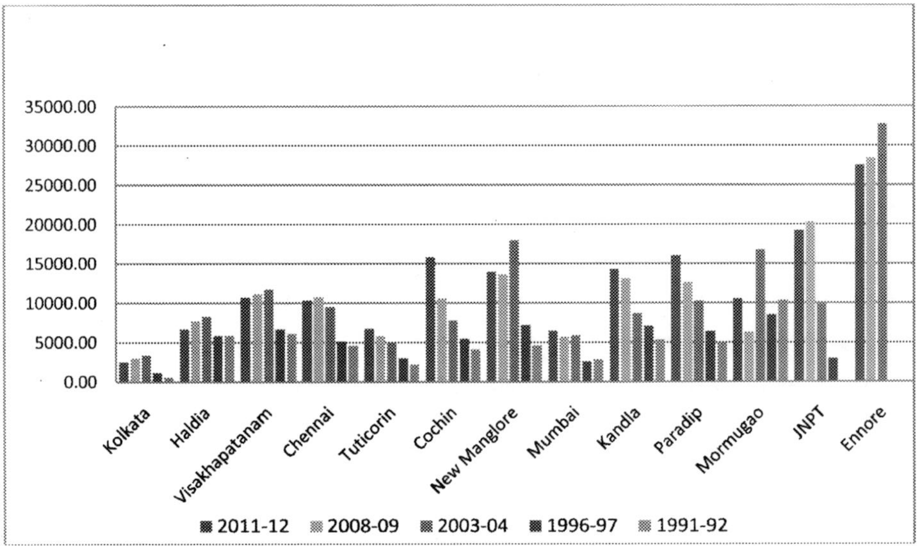

Source: Ministry of Shipping, Road Transport & Highways, Govt. of India.

2.7 Volume of Cargo Handled at Major Ports of India (1991–2012) (in MT)

An analysis of the cargo handled at the 12 major ports of India reveals that the Kandla Port has handled the largest share of cargo followed by Visakhapatnam and the JNPT. A low account of cargo handling was reported at the port of Ennore, not because of poor performance, but because of lower capacity. A detailed analysis of cargo handling has already been done in the chapter Port Traffic: Composition and Volume.

Table 2.16: Volume of Cargo Handled at the Major Ports of India (1991–2012) (in MT)

Name of the Major Port	*Volume of Cargo Handled (in MT)*				
	2011-12	*2008-09*	*2003-04*	*1996-97*	*1991-92*
Kolkata	12.23	12.43	8.69	6.02	4
Haldia	31.01	41.79	32.57	17.1	12
Visakhapatanam	67.42	63.91	47.74	34.5	21.52
Chennai	55.71	57.49	36.71	31.85	25.05
Tuticorin	28.11	22.01	13.68	9.18	5.87
Cochin	20.09	15.23	13.57	11.74	7.48
New Mangalore	32.94	36.69	26.67	12.45	8.27
Mumbai	56.18	51.88	29.92	33.73	26.26
Kandla	82.50	72.23	41.52	33.73	21
Paradip	54.25	46.41	25.31	11.58	7.3
Mormugao	39.00	41.68	27.87	17.31	15.1
JNPT	65.75	57.29	31.27	8.07	
Ennore	14.96	11.50	9.28		

Source: Ministry of Shipping, Road Transport & Highways, Govt. of India.

Fig. 2.6: Volume of Cargo Handled at Major Ports of India (1991-2012) (in MT)

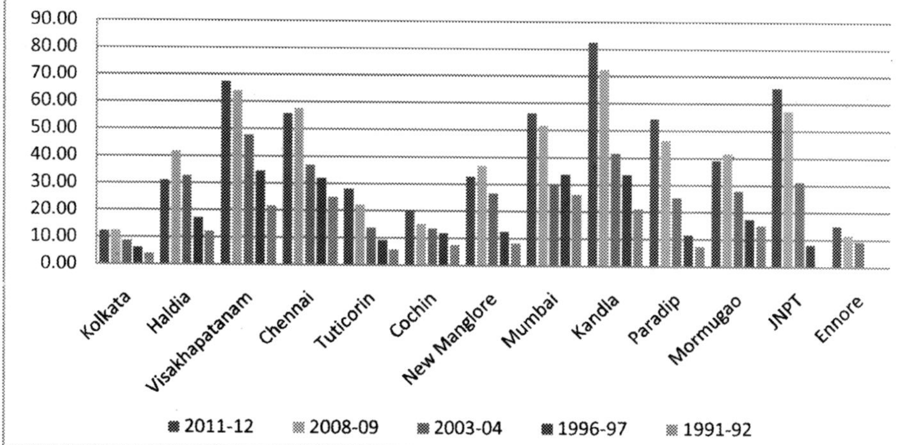

Source: Ministry of Shipping, Road Transport & Highways, Govt. of India.

2.8 The Number of Vessels Handled at the Major Ports of India (1991–2012)

The number of vessels has increased for all the ports for almost all the selected years. The maximum number of vessels was handled by the port of JNPT followed by Kandla, Visakhapatnam and Chennai. Over the years, the vessel-handling capacity has been augmented, improved as well as increased by each individual port. It is good sign for improving the conditions of the major ports of India during the post-reform era.

Table 2.17: Number of Vessels Handled at the Major Ports of India (1991–2012) (in Numbers)

Name of theMajor Port	*Number of Vessels Handled (in Numbers)*				
	2011-12	*2008-09*	*2003-04*	*1996-97*	*1991-92*
Kolkata	1204.00	856.00	765	874	717
Haldia	1962.00	1421.00	1889	947	703
Visakhapatnam	2432.00	1571.00	1704	1437	928
Chennai	2043.00	1423.00	1656	1681	1381
Tuticorin	1492.00	935.00	1517	905	724

Name of theMajor Port	*Number of Vessels Handled (in Numbers)*				
	2011-12	*2008-09*	*2003-04*	*1996-97*	*1991-92*
Cochin	557.00	831.00	1133	784	621
New Mangalore	1136.00	803.00	879	644	452
Mumbai	1579.00	1081.00	1800	2616	2106
Kandla	2714.00	1859.00	1823	1527	1022
Paradip	1328.00	973.00	1041	557	347
Mormugao	500.00	297.00	677	507	601
JNPT	2892.00	2061.00	3681	640	
Ennore	385.00	181.00	166		

Source: Ministry of Shipping, Road Transport & Highways, Govt. of India.

Fig. 2.7: Number of Vessels Handled at Major Ports of India (1991-2012) (in Numbers)

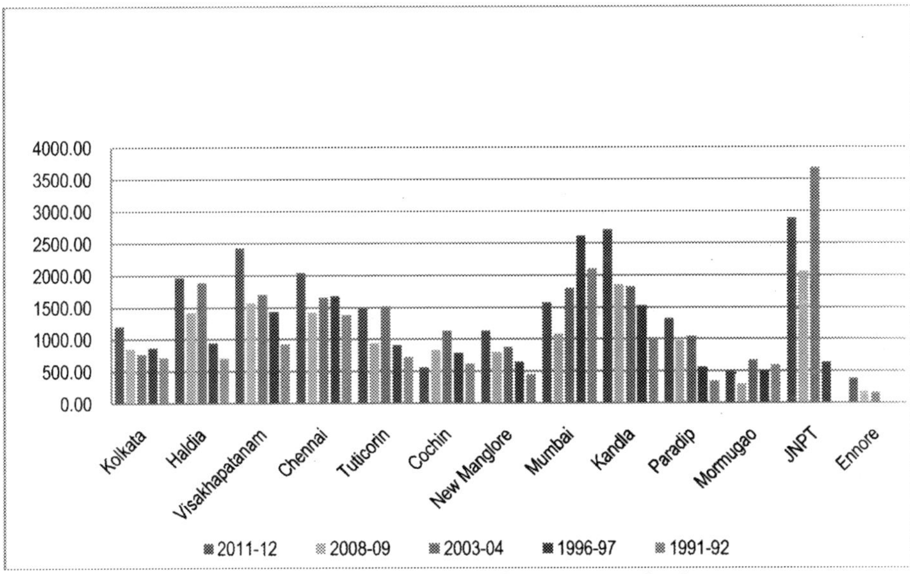

Source: Ministry of Shipping, Road Transport & Highways, Govt. of India.

2.9 Causes of the Poor Performance of Major Ports

The reasons for the slow-down in Indian port development are many. One of the main reasons is the low plan investment in the transport sector as a whole, and only a very insignificant part of it being devoted to ports over the half century after Independence. It is surprising to note that such a crucial infrastructural sub-sector like ports is the worst-affected area in terms of both allocation and utilisation of the development fund during the plans. Again, in all the plans except the Fourth, a fund utilisation in the port sector has always been marred by inefficiency. A failure in utilising the disbursed funds may have been responsible for the reduced allocation in the subsequent period. And as a matter of fact, due to this low investment, adequate capacity has not been created. In fact, the government has failed to understand the crucial role the port sector can play in the liberalised regime. But, this sort of reasoning cannot go beyond a proximate explanation. The more fundamental cause must be sought in the lack of export orientation of our investment policies starting from the Second Plan to the Ninth Plan and this is more so in a country where the ports account for more than 90 per cent of the tangible trade[7].

Apart from a low plan investment, an awareness, direction and understanding of the port industry has been lacking. The port authorities must understand both the revenue-earning capacity and the catalytic role of the ports. There is an urgent need for a coordinated policy for regulating and encouraging investments from both the public and private sectors in the port sector. One may be surprised to note that although all the 12 major ports are controlled by the Government of India through the Ministry of Surface Transport, the government still does not have a coordinated port policy. It has only some guidelines issued from time to time on an ad hoc basis. Again, some of the maritime states like Gujarat and Maharashtra have some port policies of their own but they too lack the required direction. There is no doubt that the country needs a commercial revolution in the port industry. But to do this, the Indian ports need to go through a process of technological development which demands monetary and fiscal policies which are no less than revolutionary.

Many studies reveal that although the central government and its respective maritime states have opened the sector to private investment, the experience suggests that the investors have to face an unwilling bureaucracy in getting the projects cleared. The major trouble is that quite a large number of clearances are required which are controlled by the union and state governments and there is a lack of transparency.

Another very critical factor that has accounted for poor performance in India's waterfront industry is the absence of inter-port competition which has been the source of substantial productivity increases in the national port systems in many countries.

The consequence of all these shortcomings for the Indian economy continues to be severe. In liner trades, very few carriers serve India's ports through direct calls. Because of the high costs of operation of the modern deep-sea line haul, tonnage carriers cannot accept the long waiting times at the Indian ports.

Fig. 2.8: Identified Problems of Major Ports

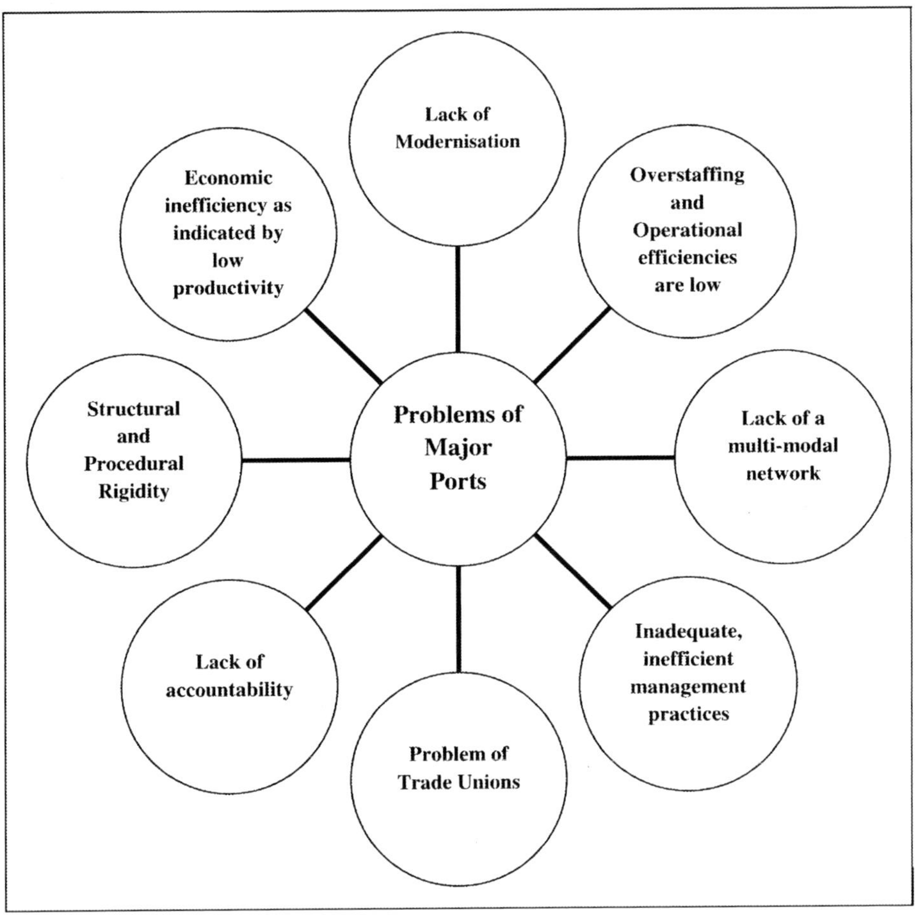

Most of the general cargo traffic, particularly container traffic, takes place though trans-shipment at Colombo, Dubai or Singapore. The extra transit time and additional costs incurred by the Indian importers and exporters are substantial. The cost of the excessive ship waiting times in ports due to slow cargo processing in the case of bulk trades are passed on to the ultimate user thereby raising the price of the imports unnecessarily and also undermine the competitiveness of the Indian exports in the international markets.

2.10 Summary of the Conclusions

A comparative analysis of the major ports in India has been done by using a Composite Index. From the above it is found that Ennore ranked first, followed by the JNPT. The analysis reveals that the overall performance of the new ports in India is comparatively better than the old ports of India except Visakhapatnam.

Geographically, the ports of eastern India have stagnated, while the same on the western and southern coasts have flourished. Contrary to conventional belief, the performance of a port has been proved to be significant depending upon the overseas cargo. An allocation of funds by both the union and state governments over the plan period has been found to be too low for utilising the potential of the huge coastline through the development of transport infrastructure.

Automation, training, service and support, spare parts, crane information management systems, preventive maintenance and integration are examples of some of the areas of focus which are to be looked into for the future. The port and terminal operators will have to implement best practices and cost-cutting initiatives; lean organisations and lean operation processes are better prepared for longer periods of decreasing volumes and rates than the ones that have not adapted.

NOTES

1 Buddhadeb Ghosh and Prabir De, "Indian Ports and Globalisation: Grounding Economics in Geography", *Economic and Political Weekly*, August 25, 2001, pp. 3271-3283.

2 Interim Report of Major Ports Reforms Committee, Ministry of Surface Transport, Department of Surface Transport, New Delhi, GOI, 1985.

3 Sasi Kumarand M. Bhasi, "A Comparative Study of Performance of India's Major Sea Ports", *Indian Ports*, Vol. 36 (2), Oct., 2004, pp.9-18.

4 M. K. Dasgupta and P. S. Mukhopadhyay, "Minor Ports of India: A Profile", *Indian Institute of Port Management,* Kolkata, 1996.

5. Ghosh and De, op. cit., p. 70.

6 Ibid.

7 Buddhadeb Ghosh and Prabir De, "Indian Ports and Globalisation: Grounding Economics in Geography", *Economic and Political Weekly*, August 25, 2001, pp.3271-3283.

3

Port Restructuring and Modernisation in the Post-Reform Era

Ever since our country embarked on the path of economic liberalisation and opened its doors to the forces of globalisation, ports have become a potential destination for wide-ranging investment and modernisation. The cumulative pressure for widespread policy-related reforms in the port sector is evident from the fact that the Government of India initiated many programmes/projects for the development of new ports. There is also a growing interest by private investors in taking up port projects and the government has encouraged private sector participation in the development of ports as infrastructure.[1]

Ports are no longer mere modal interfaces between surface transport and sea transport. They are now logistics and distribution platforms in the supply chain network. Also, the regional environment in which the ports operate, matters greatly. Ports are not isolated entities connecting to virtual value chains. They are part of a regional economy, and the evolution of the regional economy strongly affects the performance of the port. It is, therefore, important that the multifaceted structure of the port system in India is analysed and the influence that these ports have on the regional development of their hinterlands is systematically assessed.

With the growing move for privatisation and public–private

partnerships in seaports all over the world subsequent to reforms, private sector participation in the operations and infrastructure activities of the seaports has increased substantially over the last few years. This has resulted in a radical change in the organisational models of ports, from the 'Service' port model to a 'Landlord' port model.[2] In the latter, the 'port authority' retains the port infrastructure and fulfils its regulatory functions, while the port services are provided by private operators who own the assets conforming to the port's superstructure and equipment required for service provision. The ports along the long peninsular coastline of India have suddenly become the cynosure of investor and public policy attention in India.[3] This is barely surprising considering that a cumulative pressure for the widespread policy-related reforms in the port sector coupled with a growing investor interest in taking up port projects has been building up ever since the country embarked on the path of economic liberalisation and opened its doors to the forces of globalisation with the opening up of the domestic port sector to private operators. Entrusting private operators to manage certain terminals within the ports through concession agreements has led to the gradual privatisation of the major Indian ports. With the government ushering in private participation in the port development sector, concession agreements are popular features where the state governments offer a complete freedom to the private entrepreneurs to develop and operate the numerous minor ports dotting the country's coastline. During the Tenth and Eleventh Five Year Plans, it was proposed to enhance the capacity and improve the productivity of the major ports with a focus on the measures aimed at modernisation, rendering of cost-effective services, enhancement of service quality, commercialisation through corporatisation and increased private sector participation.[4]

3.1 Trends in Port Growth and Port Privatisation in India

Economic liberalisation and the globalisation process started in India since the early nineties. However, the first steps towards private sector participation in infrastructural services were taken up only in the mid-nineties. Infrastructure-related economic policy reforms in India were initiated and catalysed following the release of the Rakesh Mohan

Committee Report on Infrastructure Development in 1996, which sought a fresh policy framework for private sector involvement in the development of infrastructure-related services.[5]

The trend initially took off in Gujarat with the state government offering a slew of captive port facilities to private sector participants for the development and operation of minor and intermediate ports. Subsequently, major ports also began a wide range of development and modernisation activities, often with private sector involvement in setting up and operating terminal facilities as well as the operation of port services. In the changing scenario of the Indian port sector, it is a misnomer to treat India's minor ports as really 'minor'. They are really neither small in size nor in the terms of the traffic volumes being handled by them. With ports like Mundra and Pipavav, the private sector is getting ready to compete with the major ports.[6]

This differentiation in nomenclature was without a significant impact till liberalisation, when the government allowed private enterprise into the sector. Then, given that neither the Constitution nor the legislations defined ports by size or investment, governments like that of Gujarat took full advantage to invite and attract private enterprise into the sector. As a result of greater flexibility in decision-making and the prospect of greater revenue for the state governments, the process of privatisation reached a more advanced stage in the case of minor ports (as opposed to Public–Private Partnerships (PPPs) in major port operation and expansion). Furthermore, the state governments rather than pushing the central government for major ports in their respective states preferred to notify minor ports, inviting private developers as port operators. The states of Gujarat, Maharashtra and Andhra Pradesh, for example, launched active campaigns to attract investors and real-estate developers to their ports, often combining industrial site development projects with port investment and vice versa.[7] The current focus of the central government is largely on the expansion and increase of capacity in the existing major ports under its jurisdiction. The importance of minor and intermediate ports, however, has not diminished as their development is being aggressively pursued by every maritime state. The emerging global economy has opened up new avenues in all the sectors in general and the maritime sector in particular. The maritime sector through economic liberalisation, competition, upgraded technology and the application of modern information technology is being talked about worldwide.[8]

The Government has been encouraging private sector participation in port development since 1996. The major areas which have been thrown open for private investment, mainly on a Build, Operate and Transfer (BOT) basis with a revenue–sharing mechanism includes the construction of cargo handling berths, container terminals and warehousing facilities, installation of cargo handling equipment, construction of dry-docks and ship repair facilities, etc. The preferred route for private sector participation is through open competitive bidding.[9]

3.2 National Maritime Development Programme

The development of ports is an ongoing process based on the requirement of the trade and future projections of traffic. Projects are taken up based on the requirement of individual ports to cater to the traffic. Recognising the catalytic role which the maritime sector has to play in India's fast growing economy and in fulfilling the trade objectives, the National Maritime Development Programme (NMDP) has been formulated by the Ministry of Shipping, Govt. of India. Under the Programme, 276 projects to be taken up for implementation over the period from 01.04.2005 to 31.03.2012 have already been identified.[10]

Ports are interfaces in a complex chain of logistical stations where not only containers and general cargo but also numerous kinds of bulk goods, like coal and ores, are loaded and unloaded at maritime and river terminals, stored and transferred to power stations, agricultural and industrial centres using conveyors, road and rail transport. Therefore, the ports deal with a wide range of activities like the movement of ships, passengers, cargo/ container through different modes of transport, the loading and unloading of ships and interaction/clearance from the different statutory bodies and port users. In addition, the allocation and management of physical resources like berths, anchorage, channels, tugs, warehouses, storage space, human resources, etc. are also to be considered. Therefore, the management of a port involves an efficient deployment and utilisation of all resources, backed-up by timely and accurate information, which can be successfully achieved only by an efficient deployment of a state-of-art Information Technology.[11]

In view of the innovations in the Information and Communication Technology, the maritime industry is undergoing rapid technological changes. A high degree of automation in operations is being aimed for the ports the world over to meet the increase in demand of the efficiency of port operations. Hence, the application of Information Technology is one of the key issues in the modernisation of ports.

3.3 Mechanisation of Indian Ports: Present Status

Presently, the Indian ports are now rapidly moving towards an application of the state-of-art technology and internet technology to implement an integrated Port Operation System and to move towards a paperless regime so as to reduce the dwell time and also, the cost to the users.

Automation is aimed at through the use of:

- Vessel Traffic Management System (VTMS)
- Information Technology in Operational and non-operational areas
- Surveillance System and Safety & Security System
- Electronic Commerce (EC)/Electronic Data Interchange (EDI)

3.3.1 Vessel Traffic Management System (VTMS)

VTMS has already been installed at Mumbai, Jawaharlal Nehru, Kolkata, Chennai, Cochin, New Mangalore and Mormugao Ports. Installation of the VTMS in the Gulf of Kutch providing coverage to the port of Kandla and other non-major ports along the Gulf is under process.[12]

3.3.2 Information Technology

The Indian ports have implementing/implemented a heterogeneous system using the latest technology covering the following modules/applications for an efficient functioning of the ports:

(i) Integrated Vessel Services and Control Management
(ii) Integrated Cargo Management and Accounting System for all types of cargo (which includes import & export module, Rail/ CONCOR Operation and billing)
(iii) Integrated Container Handling and Tracking system
(iv) Resource Planning (Including Equipment, Labour, etc.)[13]

3.3.3 Surveillance System and Safety & Security System

As a result of a fallout of the 9/11 incident in the United States, a number of new technologies have been introduced to help the implementation of International Ship and Port Facility Security (ISPS) Code in various countries including India. All the major ports are ISPS compliant. In process of implementing the ISPS, the need for a biometric-based access control management was felt and many ports are in the process of implementing it.[14]

Besides, the requirement of a CCTV-based surveillance system has also been felt and some ports are also reaping the benefits of the same. Now, all crafts tend to have an AIS system, which installs a satellite station on a ship. Similarly, the use of radio frequency identification (RFID) is gaining ground in the logistics and transport planning and an optical charter recognition (OCR) is being used quite cleverly in the terminals to speed up the processing of containers in and out.[15]

It is also proposed to introduce a container scanning system in a phased manner, in addition to the introduction of an automatic surveillance system like the CCTVs. Because of a terror threat, the surveillance and security issues have become the top-most priority for the ports. Therefore, the need of a very stringent and secured RFID/smart card and biometric verification at the access points within the ports/terminals for the seaport personnel, vehicles and container truck traffic management has arisen. The ports are geared to take up this challenge. The need of an electric fencing with a breach alarm is also being thought of.[16]

3.3.4 Electronic Commerce (EC)/Electronic Data Interchange (EDI)

The members of the Port Community depend on the flow of data from the other members of the community for performing their functions effectively, since activity in one area will have an impact on the others. If data can be exchanged between them accurately and speedily, the efficiency and throughput will be improved. Electronic Data Interchange (EDI) has therefore become an essential element for maintaining the efficient operation not only of ports but also for the complete trade and transportation cycle.[17]

The EC/EDI implementation is being vigorously pursued in the functioning of the trade regulating and facilitating organisations like Customs, ports, airports, airlines, banks, DGFT, AEPC/Texprocil, CONCOR, Railways, etc. The implementation of EDI varies from port to port and covers areas like banks, exchange with Customs and few messages with few users.

3.3.5 The Way Forward: Towards a Paperless Regime

To achieve a paperless regime, the ports have to gear up with a complete automation at the individual port and Port Community levels. Each port should undertake Enterprise Resource Planning (ERP) solutions which would cover all functional areas including port operation. In the functional areas where the ERP solutions are not available on the shelf, the solutions should be developed and integrated with the ERP solutions. Ports like Cochin and Mormugao have already implemented ERP solutions along with a Port Operation System and other modules that are not part of an ERP solution. New Mangalore is in the process of implementing a similar ERP solution followed by all the other ports.[18]

Non-ERP solutions like GIS linking with the Land/Estate Policy, Hospital Management, Bespoke System like Vigilance, Legal, File Tracking, Employee Welfare, Right to Information (RTI) Act, etc. shall be implemented. The ports shall implement a Land/Estate Management solution which is completely scalable for the implementation of other business processes like Financial and Management Accounting, etc. As most of the Major Ports have an initiative for the Computerisation of Land Management process, the need of the hour is the implementation of a complete application for Real Estate Management, Utilities and Advertisements which are completely scalable for the implementation of an integrated ERP application on a decentralised basis and can be linked with the Ministries' e-governance initiatives. The provision for a Self-Service Scheme available in the system could be introduced as an employee welfare measure. Automated equipment (Cargo/Container Handling, Weight Bridges) shall also be integrated with the centralised system to avoid manual intervention. A campus cabled LAN Network system shall be undertaken covering all the automation systems and as a redundancy, a wireless LAN network shall also be considered. The IT Policy of the port should be in such a way so as to integrate all the sophisticated systems in the port in a comprehensive manner such as VTMS, AIS, RFID, CCTV, Surveillance System and other security systems.[19]

A comprehensive database needs to be developed by the ports themselves which will lead to decision-making and provide artificial intelligence. Sufficient and suitable manpower shall be placed in each port for managing the IT systems and these personnel shall be trained periodically to update their knowledge and know-how.

3.4 Port Community Level Automation

The Port Community System (PCS) is intended to integrate the electronic flow of information and function as the centralised hub for the Indian ports and other stakeholders like shipping lines/Agents, surveyors, stevedores, banks, container freight stations, Government regulatory agencies, Customs House agents, importers, exporters, CONCOR/ Railways, etc. through a common interface in a secure manner using the latest technologies.[20] Now, steps have already been taken to implement the PCS at the Non-Major Ports also. Ports like Mundra, Pipavav, Gangavaram, Dehaj have already shown an interest in implementing the PCS and have taken advance steps to integrate with it.

3.5 The Present Policy for the Ports in India

The Indian Ports Act, 1908 and the Major Port Trusts Act, 1963, govern the functioning of major ports. These Acts have enough flexibility to permit private investment in the creation and operation of port facilities. Recently, greater administrative and financial powers have been delegated to the ports. However, the increased private sector participation in the ports implies a gradual change in the role of port authorities towards modernisation and mechanisation.

Another factor in favour of the corporatisation of ports is the fact that the corporative ports which do not fall under the purview of the Major Ports Trust Acts of 1963 are exempted from regulation by the authority for the major ports and are free to fix their own tariff. Even as a corporate port, as long it remains a state-owned enterprise, subject to all the regulations and procedural restrictions on the management of public enterprises, the decision-making authority of these entities is severely restricted, particularly in the matters of capital investments and barrowings which are crucial for the exploitation of commercial opportunities.

3.5.1 The Need for the Corporatisation and Privatisation of Ports

Actually, an improvement in the productivity and efficiency of port operations is one of the challenges facing the major ports today. The Major Ports in India are suffering from under-capacity and low productivity, lack of adequate commercial orientation and a less degree of autonomy to the port management. This requires a reduction of costs as well as workforce rationalisation. Both privatisation and corporatisation are part of the attempt to increase efficiency. Corporatisation will provide an easy access to private funds— even the equity market—which is not possible now.

The Government is interested in corporatisation because it will complement its policy of economic liberalisation. It will also reduce its budgetary commitment to the Major Ports. The Port Trust Management is interested in corporatisation because of a variety of reasons; The most basic one is having a greater autonomy from Government control.[21]

3.5.2 Expectations from Corporate Ports

The new corporate entity should be able to meet the challenges of economic liberalisation and the emerging domestic and international competition in all commercial activities.

1. The new corporate entity should be able to take faster decisions in the matters of capacity expansion and modernisation.
2. It should be able to mobilise resources both internally and externally for its own growth.

It is an urgent necessity to attract a private sector investment into the port sector. It is not just a question of adding capacity. A private investment would lead to the induction of modern technology, improved management; improve efficiency and productivity and quality of service as well as bring in competitiveness in the port services.[22] Private investment till now has been fairly limited, though it has shown some interest in the last few years.[23]

3.5.3 Privatising Options

The options for privatising port services depend on the size of the port and the services involved. The models for privatising include the following:· Full privatising: all assets and liabilities are transferred to the private sector.

- *Build, operate and own*: parts of the port are sold to the private operators to be developed.
- *Build, operate and transfer*: private operators build or rehabilitate facilities, which are eventually transferred to the public ownership; also known as concessions.
- *Joint ventures*: operators create a new independent company. This type of agreement arises when two or more parties with common interests join forces.
- *Leasing*: the port authority leases port assets to private operators for a given period. In contrast with a concession, the private operators do not usually make an investment, and therefore, only assume commercial risks.
- *Licensing*: Private operators provide services requiring basic equipment, which they own. The port authority owns the port

infrastructure and super-infrastructure and charges the private operators for their use.

- *Management contract*: the port authority remains the owner of the port, but the port is run by a private firm, which can provide a more efficient management of the operations.

Fig. 3.1: The Privatisation and Efficiency Cycle

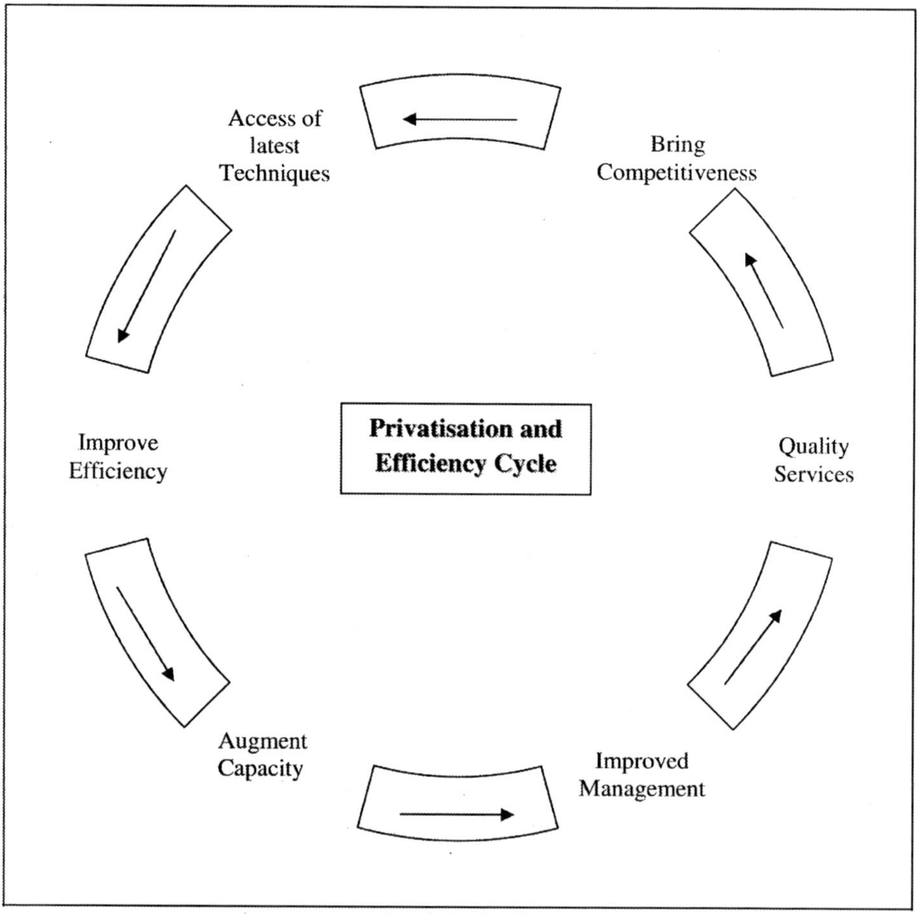

Source: Prepared on the basis of literature survey.

3.6 Guidelines on Privatisation

The guidelines have clearly identified the areas for private participation. These have included the leasing out of existing assets, construction and operation of liquid bulk, break bulk, multipurpose and specialised cargo berths, the construction and operation of container terminals, construction and operation of warehouses, CFS, storage facilities, tank farms, captive power plants, captive facilities for port-based industries and the leasing of floating crafts. Open competitive bidding was introduced along with a two-cover tender system, covering both a technical and a price bid. The main criteria for selecting the bidders were highest returns and lowest cost to the port trust. There were not many takers. In particular, foreign players were unhappy with the BOT framework. They found it difficult to raise finances in the absence of an ownership clause. The port trust gave no guarantee either of financial return or expected traffic. By the mid-1990s, the only major private player was the Australia-based P&O, which expressed an interest in developing a BOT container terminal at the JNPT.[24] After long-drawn negotiations, P&O was handled the BOT project in January 1997.

In 1997, the Ports Laws Act modified both the Indian Port Act, 1908 and the Major Port Trust Act, 1963. This also paved the way for the setting up of an independent regulatory body for setting tariff—the Tariffs Authority—for the Major Ports, which was established in 1997. Further modifications were made in the Port Policy in June 1998 to allow for the setting up of joint ventures and collaborations between a major port and company/consortium and between a major and minor port. It also allowed the ports to enter into bilateral agreements with foreign governments.

Initially, a 51 per cent FDI was allowed in the sector. In 1999, the FDI limit was increased to 100 per cent. Another significant move was the finalisation and issue of a model concession agreement in March 2000.[25] In this, the Government shares a number of risks with the investors. Despite this, private participation remains quite selective; most of the private interest is concentrated on the development of containers. Container terminals are being given to private operators on a BOT basis for a period of thirty years. Very few seem interested in cargo terminals or infrastructural facilities. The cause is obvious that containerisation can provide quick returns as compared to other infrastructures like cargo terminals which have a long-gestation period. The Minor Ports have found it comparatively easier to attract private investment.[26]

3.6.1 State Port Privatisation Policy

Gujarat has envisaged an integrated port development strategy, consisting of the creation of port facilities, industrialisation and development of infrastructure facilities like roads and railways in the hinterland. Significant to the Gujarat privatisation initiative, are the build-own-operate-transfer policy principles governing the development of these projects. The policy evolution based on a potential investor/port-user feedback reflects an objective, facilitating role for the government rather than one of direct participation.

3.6.2 Financing Agencies

However, multilateral agencies which have a larger developmental role have been involved in port financing, especially in the Greenfield projects. Amongst the multilateral agencies, the World Bank is the biggest source of aid for this sector in India. The World Bank's private arm, the International Finance Corporation (IFC), has been an active participant in providing both debt and equity. The Asian Development Bank, ANZ, Standard Chartered and HSBC are the other prominent foreign banks involved in the sector. In India, the leading domestic FIs in the area of port financing are ICICI, IDBI, IFCI and IDFC.[27] These have been more active in funding private port projects such as Dhamra (ICICI), Adani (IFCI) and Pipavav (IDBI). Domestic banks such as Canara Bank also provide loans to the port projects, mostly in conjunction with the domestic FIs. The promoters of the SPV companies are usually foreign and domestic ports, shipping agents, stevedoring companies, construction companies, O&M companies, shipping lines or other companies involved in the port sector. Foreign companies are allowed to hold 100 per cent equity in the SPV company. Some of the foreign companies operating in the port sector in India are P&O Ports (of Australia), PSA, Stevedoring Services of the US, Maersk Shipping and Precious Shipping of Thailand. Several multilateral agencies have also contributed to the equity in the SPVs. These are ADB (which is likely to pick up equity in Ennore) and CDC of the UK (in Pipavav).

The modernisation of the port infrastructure is essential for benchmarking the performance of the Indian ports as against global standards. The Government of India has given a top priority to the modernisation of ports, which is being undertaken through:

- Construction of new berths/terminals
- Various expansion/upgradation projects for berths
- Installation of new and modern equipment
- Upgradation/replacement through higher capacity of cargo handling equipment
- Mechanisation of cargo-handling operations
- Various computer-aided systems to encourage automation in port operation
- Installation of Vessel Traffic Management System (VTMS) for a smooth movement of vessels
- Implementation of a Web-based Port Community system

3.7 A Policy Framework for the Development and Modernisation of Ports

In order to augment the capacity and to enhance the productivity levels at the Major ports, several initiatives in the form of guidelines and policies have been taken in the recent past as explained in the succeeding paragraphs.

3.7.1 Expansion of Berth Capacities

The Public–Private Partnership (PPP) mode is the preferred mode of implementation of all the new berth projects. Port projects are awarded through a competitive bidding process on the revenue sharing model. In addition, requests from the port-based industries for the construction and operation of facilities for captive use are being considered on a case-to-case basis.

3.7.2 Mechanisation

The mechanisation of the cargo-handling facilities is of utmost importance for improving the efficiency of ports. The introduction of high capacity mechanised equipments in the form of mobile harbour cranes/floating cranes, etc is required. Private sector participation is being encouraged, with a view to utilising the latent capacity as well as for augmenting the cargo-handling capacity of the Major Ports, which would go a long way in reducing the handling cost of cargo at the Major Ports and will also increase the throughput substantially.

3.7.3 Development and Maintenance of Channels

One of the most important features of the modern and more efficient ports is to have a deep drafted channel to accommodate and navigate the longer vessels. Towards this objective, the ports are required to undertake capital and maintenance dredging in the channel on a regular basis. Presently, most of the dredging requirements of the Major Ports, particularly maintenance dredging, are being met by the Dredging Corporation of India. As per the present Dredging Policy, the Indian dredging companies have the right of first refusal if their offer falls within 10 per cent of the lowest technically qualified bid.

3.7.4 Port Connectivity

All the Major Ports in the country are at present having both road and rail connectivity. However, the capacity and quality of the existing connectivity require improvement so that the flow of cargo in and out of the port is smooth and efficient. The projects on rail and road connectivity are being implemented mainly by the National Highways Authority of India (NHAI) and the Railways, respectively. In a number of instances, the ports have made a significant financial contribution for the execution of the road and rail connectivity projects.

3.7.5 Electronic Data Interchange-Port Community System (EDI-PCS)

As a part of Electronic Data Interchange, a Centralized Web Based-Port Community System (PCS) has been introduced at all the Major Ports with a view to transforming the Indian ports into modern Ports and for minimising the transaction time and cost to the Indian export–import trade. Computerisation by way of the Port Community System includes a uniform and centralised web-based message exchange hub covering all the stakeholders including ports, customs, banks, railways, Mercantile

Marine Department (MMD), Port Health Organisation, Container Corporation of India (CONCOR), port users, etc. the PCS has heralded a paperless regime in the Indian port business. The PCS having implemented in the Major Ports, will be extended to Non-Major Ports within a set time frame.

This will greatly reduce the scope of human interface in the delivery of services, enable a single-window facility, reduce multiple transactions and ensure that the port users do not have to visit the port for transacting routine business. The PCS will be fully implemented when the Customs gets linked with the System. The implementation of the PCS with its integration with the Customs is expected to reduce a transaction cost at the ports and empower the Indian ports to join the premier league of international technologically advanced e-ports.

3.7.6 Land Policy

The land available with the ports is one of the essential and significant resources for sustainable growth. It is an established practice globally for the ports to allot land for carrying out economic activity including establishing industry to ensure a captive cargo to the port, thereby enhancing the sustainability of that port. An optimum utilisation of land is a matter of continuing importance to all ports. Keeping in mind their specific requirements, ports have to leverage their assets including their real estate within the framework of the Master Plan for the Port. The ports may allot their land on license, short lease and long lease up to a 30-year period, depending upon the nature of the port-related activities, by following a competitive bidding process. The port lands have also been used to set up Special Economic Zones (SEZs) aimed at encouraging industrial development in and around the port.In addition to the existing framework of policy and the initiatives taken up during the recent past, the Ministry has constituted a high level committee to look into the various policies impinging upon the growth of this sector, especially in the background of recession and down-turn and the Committee has made its recommendations on each of the aspects of port management. These recommendations are under examination by the Ministry and the existing policies will be modified/improvised as and when considered necessary.

NOTES

1 Sadanand Gupta, "Restructuring of Major Ports in India in the Post Reform Era (1991-2004)" MPhil Dissertation, Unpublished, 2005, CSRD/SSS/JNU, New Delhi.
2 http://www.oecd.org/countries/mongolia/42228028.pdf.
3 http://www.unmillenniumproject.org/documents/MainReportComplete-lowres.pdf.
4 Sudarshan Rodriguez and Aarthi Sridhar, "Harbouring Trouble", The Social and Environmental Upshot of Port Growth in India, *Dakshin Foundation*, 2010.
5 Arpita Mukherjee, Divya Satija, Ramneet Goswami, Smita Miglani and Tanu M. Goyal, "Enhancing Bilateral Trade, Investment and Collaboration in Services: India and European Union", Konrad Adenauer Stiftung (KAS), November 2012.
6 Op.cit., Sudarshan Rodriguez and Aarthi Sridhar.
7 Ibid.
8 M. Raman, (2004), "Corporatization of Ports: It is the Way Forward?" *Indian Ports*, Jan, Vol. 35 (3), pp. 5-6.
9 L. Lakshmanan, "Public-Private Partnership in Indian Infrastructure Development: Issues and Options", http://www.rbi.org.in/scripts/BS_VIEWContent.aspx?ID=1912.
10 Maritime Agenda (2010-2020), Ministry of Shipping, Government of India, January, 2011.
11 Ibid.
12 Ibid.
13 Ibid.
14 Ibid.
15 Ibid.
16 Ibid.
17 Ibid.
18 Ibid.
19 Ibid.
20 www.csi-vizag.org/LinkClick.aspx?
21 J. Sarkar (2002), "Principle of Traffic forecasting", *Indian Ports*, July, pp.9-12.
22 "Privatisation Policy for Ports", *Indian Infrastructure*, June 2004, p. 28.
23 "Port Sector: Coping With Growth" *Indian Infrastructure*, July 2001, p.22.
24 K.V.A. Iyer (2004), "Refining Seaport Privatisation: Indian Experience", *Indian Ports*, Jan., pp. 19-23.
25 "Privatisation Policy for Ports", *Indian Infrastructure*, June 2004, p. 28.
26 "Ports of Future", *Geography and You*, Vol.3 (9), Sep., 2003, pp. 31-32.
27 "Port Financing: Still a Trickle", *Indian Infrastructure*, July 2001, pp.28-29.

4

Containerisation of Ports: Issues and Implications

"Containerization is the use of containers to unitize cargo for transportation, supply and storage". Container logistics thus incorporates supply, transportation, packaging, storage and security together with the visibility of the container and its contents into a distribution system from the source to the user. Ports, railways, roads, warehouses, shipping and logistics companies by virtue of being the primary players dealing with the containers are also the key contributors to the development of the container trade and infrastructure.[1]

The advancement in overall trade and benefits due to the adoption of the containers for transport has brought forward the term "Trading in the Box". Containerisation thus, in trade terms, is the driver of various players towards the utilisation of containers for transporting goods between various places and by various modes of transport.

There are various container types catering to different needs:

- General purpose dry cargo containers for boxes, cartons, cases, sacks, bales, pallets, drums in standard, high or half height
- High cube purpose container, which is a 40 foot container of 9′6″ height. It is recommended for light voluminous cargoes which would otherwise not fit in a normal 8′ height container

- Refrigerated or reefer containers
- Open top containers for bulk minerals, heavy machinery
- Open side for loading oversize pallet
- Flush folding flat-rack containers for heavy and bulky semi-finished goods, out of gauge cargo
- Platform or bolster for barrels and drums, crates, cable drums, out of gauge cargo, machinery and processed timber
- Insulated Containers for perishable goods (fruits, vegetables, etc.) which require protection from temperature change without the necessity of refrigeration
- Ventilated containers for organic products requiring ventilation
- Tank containers for bulk liquids and dangerous goods
- Rolling floor for difficult-to-handle cargo
- Collapsible or folding flat rack containers
- Bulk containers for grain, fertilisers, chemicals, etc. in bulk. It is fitted with manholes to facilitate the bulk cargo through gravity
- Garment containers are fitted with hangers to help loading a large number of garments in hangers inside the container
- Pen container for cattle or livestock. It has netted windows on the side or ends to facilitate ventilation. On the lower part of the side walls, it has cleaning and drainage outlets.

The advantages of containerisation are well known throughout the port industry. Few of them are as follows:

(a) Effective handling of cargo (specially liquid cargo)
(b) Minimal or no damage to goods
(c) Optimum utilisation of storage and warehousing capacity
(d) Technology adoption due to mechanised handling required for handling containers
(e) Skill development of workers for operating containers
(f) Reduction in transport time
(g) Door-to-door or end-to-end delivery of goods, etc.

In addition, containers enhance the effectiveness of the overall supply chain mechanism in the trade.

4.1 Containers and Port System

The container traffic at major ports has almost doubled in the last 5–6 years. Container traffic in India at the Major Ports has shown growth at an average rate of 13–15 per cent per year. Globally, the container traffic has grown at around 10 per cent in the past 20 years. This showcases the consolidated position of the Indian container industry vis-à-vis the world. According to an estimate, the world container throughput will reach 1 billion TEUs by 2020, which is almost double of the current container traffic. The emerging Asian and African countries are expected to be the prime movers in achieving this growth.[2]

India is going to be the preferred destination for a global manufacturing hub. This fact presents many opportunities for the ports to change their current operation style and be ready for the foreseen surge in the demand for handling and faster evacuation of containers. Many investments have been proposed and steps have been taken by the various port authorities for attracting the container traffic.

4.2 Containerised Cargo Commodities

The major cargo commodities that get containerised are garments, electronic goods, agro-products, cotton yarn, machinery parts, granite products, coir products, leather products and jute products. The Indian ports have also been seeing many hitherto break-bulk cargoes like rice, maize, glass, granite, garnet sand, sugar, soya, cement and flowers which are now moving in containers.

Some break-bulk cargo such as banana, cotton and green coffee beans have become permanent container fixtures, while others such as pulp, lumber, cocoa and onions migrate from container to ship holds and back to containers, according to the rise and fall of box rates. Even iron ore has been successfully exported from Chennai in containers. All this points to a steady move towards containerisation for its value-added benefits. The main beneficiary would be the container shipping industry and container terminals.

In addition, with regard to cost economics, the handling cost is lower for containerised cargo as opposed to break bulk leading to the containerisation of the minerals exported. With the imports being 40 per cent more than the exports, the incoming containers wait for repositioning to other locations. Container lines, instead of spending on shipping out empties, offer good deals for shippers to specific locations as a result of which soya, sugar, steel plates and agricultural products have gone the container way.

4.3 Policies and Trends in Containerisation

The success of any sector or industry depends upon both the private players and the Government authorities. Accordingly, the success of the infrastructure sector or containerisation as a sub-set cannot be attributed to the efforts of a single side. Policies and regulations thus play an important part in the development of container infrastructure. An assessment of the salient features of the various policy and regulations affecting the development of container infrastructure and in turn the growth of the container progress in India is given in the subsequent paragraphs.

4.4 Policies Affecting Containerisation

4.4.1 Foreign Direct Investment

One of the parameters for judging the maturity of a country's trade and industry is the development of infrastructure. While relaxing the norms for foreign investments in India, the Indian government also has considered the infrastructural requirements and thus opened the infrastructure sector to investments. The development of infrastructure is of prime importance to the containerisation drive. In the transport infrastructure sector, there are no restrictions on investment. Following are the salient features of the FDI policy on the transport infrastructure sector:

1. 100 per cent FDI in maritime infrastructure like ports, terminals, jetties, harbours, merchant shipbuilding;
2. 100 per cent FDI in support infrastructure like warehousing, roads, inland water transport, other logistics components.

Trade growth, penetration of containerisation and a hub-and-feeder service structure are the drivers of the container traffic growth. Presently, containerised cargo represents about 35–40 per cent of India's external trade by value, and this proportion is likely to grow as containerisation increasingly penetrates the general cargo trades and increases its share. Looking at the container traffic growth in the past few years, there seems to be a scope for hub operations in India. Further, shipping trends will play an important role in deciding whether the Indian ports have a potential for hub operations. Hinterland connectivity is a critical area to ensure a seamless flow of containers and improved port productivity. Currently, more than 30 per cent of the traffic is expected to move hinterland by rail and the remaining is expected to move entirely by road, mostly to nearby Container Freight Stations (CFSs), and some to the interior Inland Container Depots (ICD). There are also issues with respect to the evacuation of containers from the ICDs. There is a lot of road-based congestion due to insufficient infrastructure. Interfacing with the customs is another issue.

The compounded annual growth rate (CAGR) of container traffic in the TEUs for the period 2001–12 was much higher than the global average for this period. Given the growing economy and international trade, a lot of future potential is being seen in this sector. This however would be contingent on the maritime sector being equipped to take the challenges emerging from (i) large shipping vessels and deeper draft at ports (ii) hub-and-feeder operations at ports and along the coast, respectively (iii) hinterland connectivity between port and Inland Container Depot (ICD)/ Container Freight Station (CFS) and (iv) terminal development on ports and in the hinterland. Other issues relate to the use of Information Technology (IT) and better systems to coordinate with bodies like the Customs and industrial location policy (especially with respect to the SEZs.

As part of the study conducted by I-Maritime and IPA (in May 2006), the container traffic will be 20.9 mTEUs (low estimate) and 24.1 mTEUs (high estimate) in 2015–16. As per the National Maritime Development Programme (NMDP) forecast, the container traffic was supposed to increase at 18.3 per cent per annum over the decade 2004–14 with the major ports having a 72 per cent share.[3]

4.4.2 Physiological Considerations for Containerisation

Colombo, for example, one of the main hubs for trans-shipping the Indian container cargo, has a draft of 15 metres. This is proposed to be increased further to 17 metres and eventually 20 metres. JNPT, the largest container port in the country, has a draft of only 12 metres. The JNPT currently handles vessels of up to 4,000 TEUs compared to 8,500 TEUs at Colombo. Despite handling a higher volume of traffic than Colombo, the JNPT is constrained by its deficient draft from offering cheaper and higher quality services, i.e. higher frequency and lower transit times. Other ports in the region like Singapore, Dubai, Port Klang, etc. have drafts of at least 15 metres and can accommodate vessels up to 11,000 TEUs.

Based on commercial criteria, the JNPT would be the logical choice for a hub port on the west coast. However, from an infrastructural perspective, neither does the JNPT have the draft for the current (and future) generation vessels nor the evacuation capability. Mundra is better placed as far as draft is concerned. As far as evacuation is concerned, while the JNPT is congested, significant investments for evacuation capacity are on the anvil. On the other hand, Visakhapatnam is the most viable port for hub operations on the eastern coast. It is in the centre of the India's eastern coast, and can even service Bangladesh and Myanmar. It has a natural water depth of 20 metres within a nautical mile from the coast due to which there is a minimal capital dredging requirement. The sea drift there is such that the maintenance dredging requirements are also less.

4.5 Drivers of Container Traffic

The growth of container traffic is driven by the following factors:

- International trade growth
- Penetration of containerisation
- Hub-and-feeder service structure
- International trade growth

Given the container traffic growth in the past few years, there seems to a scope for hub operations in India, possibly one on each coast. The absence of a hub port means that a significant share of containers leaving an Indian port goes through a feeder, trans-shipment and mainline movement. This implies an additional delay due to the feeder voyage from India to the hub port and then at the hub port while it waits for the mainline ship to call.[4] In the absence of a hub port in India, a majority of the country's containers are currently trans-shipped through other ports i.e., Colombo (just south of India), Singapore (east), Dubai and Salalah (west)[5].

The reasons for a hub port not evolving in India are:

(i) Insufficient traffic
(ii) Cabotage law
(iii) Insufficient infrastructure including draft requirement for a mainline ship

The advantages of having a hub port in India would be:

- Feeder time to the other ports would reduce
- The revenue from the trans-shipment will remains with India
- The marine side traffic from and to the hub port will move faster and cheaper.

It is interesting to note that the share of the global throughput of the top 20 ports was 75.9 per cent in 1970. It dropped to 49.6 per cent in 1980, obviously due to a proliferation of the container ports. However, since then, the share of the top 20 ports has been increasing in a marginally steady manner to reach 56.3 per cent in 2006, showing the trend of concentration due to trans-shipment and scale of economies in the bigger ports. The market for hub services is highly dependent on the patterns of ocean container trade and a specific port's location. Perhaps even more important is the economics of the trans-shipment business. The rates for trans-shipping containers are relatively low. In addition, there is little if any loyalty among customers and a carrier can easily exit the terminal at short notice, giving it a high degree of bargaining power. Ideally, the line-haul carrier should have a long-term stake in the facility to ensure its viability.[6]

4.6 Hinterland Connectivity

Hinterland connectivity is probably the most critical area for ensuring a seamless flow of containers and improved port productivity. It is an essential part of a world-class logistics system that India needs to develop with a strategic focus. The JNPT is the most efficient container port in the country and is the preferred port for a majority of the country's container traffic, presently accounting for more than 57 per cent of the total cargo handling. The east coast ports not only take much longer, but also cost more than twice as much in inland haulage charges. These differences restrict competition, and the JNPT therefore enjoys a dominant position on account of both its better overall shipping service offerings and its superior hinterland connectivity. The Gujarat ports on the other hand, continue to lose out to the JNPT due to their relatively poor connectivity, despite enjoying a closer proximity to the north-western hinterland which generates a majority of the container traffic. Even the cargo destined for China or other South-East Asian countries is preferred to be routed through the JNPT, rather than the ports like Chennai on the east coast which though closer to the destination, offer a poor connectivity to the northern hinterland.[7]

4.6.1 The Role of Railways and Roads in the Development of Port Connectivity

Currently, 35–40 per cent of the JNPT traffic is expected to move hinterland by rail while the remaining moves entirely by road, mostly to the nearby CFSs, and some to the interior ICDs. The rail capacity is barely sufficient to meet the current demand. Presently, for instance, it is estimated that the transport cost of a container from Delhi to the Mumbai Port is almost half the total logistics costs of delivering it to a destination in Europe. Inadequate capacities in the hinterland transport modes often lead to higher costs and delays on account of sub-optimal mode choices, circuitous routing and congestion in the hinterland transport links.

The Tughlakabad–JNPT (Delhi–Mumbai) line, one of the most highly trafficked corridors in the country, is a case in point. With an average line capacity of 50 trains per day, it has been handling over 67 trains per day, operating at a capacity utilisation of 135 per cent and with several sections being operated at 160 per cent utilisation levels. Roughly, 40 trains on this corridor are passenger trains, leaving a limited capacity for freight trains, which have a lower priority. Congestion at the railways' Tughlakabad ICD near Delhi and on the line itself has resulted in a poor reliability of service, and high value cargo such as containers, which form the majority of the traffic on this corridor, is increasingly shifting to road transport. Presently, less than one-third of the containerised cargo in this corridor is being carried by the Railways. On an average, 9,000 loaded trucks move over this corridor every day, aggregating around 30 MT annually of road freight traffic.[8]

4.7 Container Infrastructure Development at Ports

Ports provide an interface between ocean transport and land-based transport. India's port infrastructure constitutes of 13 Major Ports and more than 187 Non-Major Ports. Of the Non-Major Ports, only about one-fourth is operational; the rest are only fishing harbours. While the Non-Major Ports contribute significantly to the overall traffic, the containerisation traffic mostly belongs to the Major Ports. Only selected non-major/intermediate ports like Pipavav Port, Mundra Port, etc. cater to the containerised traffic. In other words, container infrastructure and trade are untapped by the Non-Major Ports. The reason may be the drafts required for the large container ships or the major investments required for the containerisation process.

Dedicated container terminals have been constructed across almost all the Major Ports to cater to the demand of container traffic. Private players have set up the CFSs/ICDs in proximity of the Major Ports. The growth of container traffic is primarily dependent on items like capital & engineering goods, textiles and food items which are transported in containers. The various Major Ports have proposed to invest in the infrastructure for the development of containerised traffic.

The transportation infrastructure works as a catalyst for the economic betterment of any country. A better transportation network in a country leads to a faster movement of goods and services, resulting into a higher turnover of goods and an increase in the GDP. Connectivity to the hinterland is of prime importance for boosting the container trade. Adequately planned schedules, a well-synchronised intermodal network and an availability of end-to-end connectivity to the prime destinations or consumption centres improve the distribution network and reduce the transit time. The roads and railways form an invaluable part of the connectivity network of the Indian Transport System. The IWT in India is not well developed and is also not available for the last mile connectivity. Thus, the Indian goods transport has to rely a lot on the roads and railways for the end-to-end delivery of goods.

The Government of India has taken up the challenge to form a dedicated network of highways and railway lines through various schemes and plans. The Expressway and the Golden Quadrilateral are some of the examples of the highway network development initiatives while the Dedicated Freight Corridor is representative of the efforts by the Ministry of Railways. Additionally, the Indian Railways and the Railway Ministry have set out quite a few policies like the Private Freight Terminals policy, etc. for enabling the container infrastructure set-up.

4.8 Container Freight Stations and Inland Container Depot Infrastructure

CFSs and ICDs form a key part of the logistics industry infrastructure. CFSs are also termed as Dry Ports in the Western countries. A CFS/ICD/ Dry Port can be defined as a "Common user facility with public authority status equipped with fixed installations and offering services for handling and temporary storage of import/export laden and empty containers carried under customs control. Transshipment of cargo can also take place from such stations."

4.8.1 Distinction between CFS and ICDs

1. In terms of functions, there is no particular distinction between a CFS and an ICD. Both cater to the transit facilities offering containerisation of break bulk cargo and vice versa. These are served by rail and road transport.

2. ICDs are generally located in the interiors or outside the port towns of the country—distant from the ports. The CFS, on the other hand, is an off-dock facility located near the port area. It is largely expected to deal with break bulk cargo originating/terminating in the immediate hinterland of port. It also deals with rail-borne traffic to and from the inland locations.
3. Considering the requirements of the Customs Act and the need to

introduce clarity in the nomenclature, all containers terminal facilities in the hinterland are designated as "ICDs".

4.8.2 Functions of the CFSs/ICDs

The primary functions of the ICD/CFS may be summed up as under:

(a) Receipt and dispatch/delivery of cargo
(b) Stuffing and stripping of containers
(c) Transit operations by rail/road to and from the serving ports
(d) Customs clearance
(e) Consolidation and desegregation of LCL cargo
(f) Temporary storage of cargo and containers
(g) Reworking of containers
(h) Maintenance and repair of container units

4.8.3 Benefits of CFSs/ICDs

The benefits as envisaged from an ICD/CFS are:

(i) Concentration points for long distance cargoes and their unitisation
(ii) Service as a transit facility
(iii) Customs clearance facility available near the centres of production and consumption
(iv) Reduced level of demurrage and pilferage
(v) No Customs required at gateway ports
(vi) The issuance of a thorough bill of lading by the shipping lines, hereby resuming a full liability of the shipments
(vii) Reduced overall level of empty container movement
(viii) Competitive transport cost
(ix) Reduced inventory cost
(x) Increased trade flows

4.9 Advent of Containerisation in India

Much before containerisation came to the Indian source, mayhem, congestion, delays and chaos prevailed at the Indian ports. It was only when containerisation made a low key entry in the early seventies that a sense of order began to rule across the ports. The sheer convenience and speed of moving cargo in containers spelt the decline of break bulk shipping. Globalisation and the opening up of the Indian economy were the next big changes. The international trade skyrocketed and Indian ports soon found themselves struggling to cope with the surge in cargo. Soon, the ports realised that in order to keep up with this speedier way of moving cargo by boxes and the demands of a booming economy, they would have to reinvent themselves and step up the pace. Taking a cue from the several international ports that had privatised their operations, India too opened its doors to usher in privatisation.

Containerisation started in India in 1973 in a humble way and since then, the container traffic has been recording an impressive leap particularly since 1992–1993, in tune with the increasing use of the containers for all types of cargoes in the international trade. With subsequent globalisation, the liberalisation of the economy and its induction into the global economy, a greater stress was put on the major Indian ports. In the last twenty years, containerisation has gained an increasing popularity; container terminals are efficient and easy to operate. The turnaround time is much lower. The containers also integrate easily with the other transport modes. Globally, as much as 80 per cent of all the maritime cargo, that is, around 200 TEUs, is transported in containers.

The real increase in containerisation actually took place in the last decade (in the 1990s) when India added about 1.76 million TEUs to the total handled cargo. Interestingly, from 2000–2001 to 2003–2004, India added about 1.5 million TEUs. Actually, the container traffic in India has grown quickly because new sites are being offered for the development of terminals. Break bulk or conventional terminals are also being converted into container mode.

This has provided trade with ample facilities and enough choice to route its cargo through any gateway port and the market forces can decide the route of the cargo, which depends on factors like the availability of services (direct or trans-shipment), cost (freight and port) and frequency. The ever-increasing numbers of containers being handled at the private terminals show that privatisation works and it is an accepted fact that privatisation has even pushed the public sector into a competitive mode.

More global players have not only brought along huge investments into the port sector, but also their expertise, experience, technology and state-of-the-art equipments.

In addition to a partnership model, some of the main issues that needed to be addressed in regard to privatisation were the multiple choices in the terms of facilities as well as port operators for the trade, review of tariffs and profits for facilitating private port development, focus on surrounding infrastructure (break-water, storage-area, warehouses, etc.) and attention to connectivity infrastructure.

With the sudden surge in container traffic, it is pivotal for the other infrastructures like road and rail to keep up with the pace and avoid traffic bottlenecks, which is very often the case at the Indian ports. An integrated service orientation of the Indian ports can be developed through enhanced infrastructural linkages. There has been an overall effort to improve the rail connectivity with various programmes being launched in this regard. The doubling of railway tracks is being undertaken wherever required. For example, the links from the JNPT to Panvel as well as from Paradip and Haldia are being doubled.

The railways have also under taken the laying of new tracks to improve the connectivity; simultaneously, the conversion of narrow gauge into broad gauge is also being undertaken. Another effort at improving the rail connectivity is the proposal to have a dedicated rail corridor for freight movement.

The annual growth for container volumes being handled by the Chennai Port till 2009–10 was 13 to 14 per cent, while the average annual container growth in the Indian ports is in the order of 8 per cent. The growth increased to 25 per cent during 2010–11; the largest growth rate among the top three container ports comprising the JNPT, Chennai and Tuticorin. This was primarily due to a capacity addition with the second terminal commencing operations coupled with the new services starting to call at the Chennai Port. The port currently has the capacity to handle 3,000,000 TEUs and with the commissioning of the third mega container terminal being planned, the capacity would go up to 8,000,000 TEUs.

Sea-land, which was established in 1957, was the first shipping company to successfully use containerisation on a mass scale. The most important benefit of containerisation was that it expedited the loading and discharging of ships, which, in turn led to an improvement in efficiency as well as an increase in trade volumes. Containers were the facilitators of inter-model transportation i.e. the movement of goods from one mode to another without the necessity of unloading and reloading. Gradually, cargoes that used to be shipped in break-bulk started getting increasingly containerised and containerisation soon became a global phenomena.

4.10 Containerisation of the Indian Ports

Necessity is the mother of invention and the invention of containerisation was perhaps the outcome of the need for a more systematic and expeditious way to handle huge amounts of cargo, lower transit times and savings on cargo contamination, damages and insurance premiums.

The growth of container traffic mainly depends on items like capital and engineering goods, textiles and food items which are essentially carried in containers. The demand for capital and engineering goods is expected to increase with infrastructural development. This, coupled with the higher exports of foodgrains and textile, is likely to drive the container traffic in the country. Further, an increase in the containerisation of bulk cargo is expected over the next few years. The container traffic at the Indian ports can be seen growing at a CAGR of 10.9 per cent, from 106.4 million tonnes in 2008–09 to 171.4 million tonnes in 2013–14. Container traffic at the Major Ports is likely to have grown at a CAGR of 7.9 per cent from 93 million tonnes to 136 million tonnes in this five-year period. Container traffic at the Non-Major Ports was expected to grow at a higher CAGR of 26.4 per cent, from 13 million tonnes to 43 million tonnes, from 2008–09 to 2013–14.

Container capacities coming up at the Pipavav, Hazira, Kulpi, Dighi and Krishnapatnam ports would primarily drive the higher container traffic growth at the Non-Major Ports. The share of the Non-Major Ports in the total containerised traffic was expected to rise from 12.5 per cent to 24 per cent in the 5-year period. If the assumed CAGR of 9 per cent as indicated by CRISIL is taken into consideration, the traffic by 2020 by Major and Non-Major Ports will reach at the level of 1955.49 million tonnes.

Table 4.1: Container Traffic (1980–81 to 2011–12)

Port	*1980-81*	*1990-91*	*2000-01*	*2010-11*	*2011-12*
Kolkata	5.34	8.54	8.74	7.94	7.56
Visakhapatnam	0.00	0.00	0.86	2.26	3.52
Chennai	7.55	17.54	17.90	25.81	25.12
Tuticorin	0.00	0.00	4.87	7.17	7.71
Cochin	12.71	4.29	5.56	3.77	3.83
New Mangalore	0.00	0.00	0.06	0.50	0.54
Mumbai	74.40	61.65	13.54	0.57	0.46
JNPT	0.00	0.00	44.31	49.50	48.64
Kandla	0.00	7.98	3.99	2.27	2.33
Paradip	0.00	0.00	0.02	0.05	0.09
Murmagao	0.00	0.00	0.14	0.16	0.19
All Ports	100.00	100.00	100.00	100.00	100.00

Source: Basic Port Statistics of India, MOST, GOI.

Containerisation is considered as the single-most important indicator of port performance. Earlier, it was part of the physical performance indicators but now it reflects the economic and infrastructural condition of a port. It measures the overall physical condition of a port. The Indian ports are less containerised as compared to the global average. The reasons behind less containerisation lie in the fact that most of the ports handle diversified commodities for the purpose of domestic and export supply. Diversification prohibits containerisation and reduces the performance of a port. Therefore, the specialisation of commodity handling by a port may substantially enhance the working capacity at a port. An integrated network of rail routes and rail infrastructure to the port system is an essential element for containerisation. Overall, rail-to-port linkages are weak in India. In addition to this, the socio-economic profile of the country is a bigger hindrance to port containerisation. Unless the profile of the Indian economy changes, it would be a difficult task for the ports to modernise themselves. Modernisation and expansion programmes are purely an outcome of economic transformation. Hence, containerisation in India must be overviewed in its totality and in fact, this is the reason that the ports of the developed countries are more containerised.

Figure 4.1: Container Traffic (1980-81 to 2011-12)

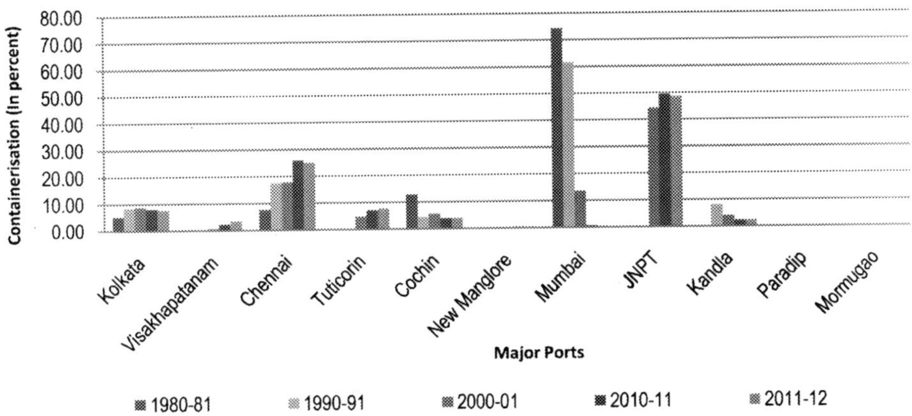

Source: Basic Port Statistics, MOST, GOI and Indian Ports Association (IPA) Report.

Containerisation is an ever-increasing element of the Indian ports. Though, containerisation was started in a limited mode and manner in 1973 in the ports of Chennai, Cochin and Mumbai. Over the years, it has been observed that newly developed ports have been the more preferred designations for port containerisation owing to suitability and infrastructural advantages. After an overview of the facts, one can make out that the newly created ports, either major or minor, are performing better that the old ones. The JNPT is the most containerised port of India; it accounts for more than half (57 per cent) of the commodities through the means of containerisation. During 1980–81, Mumbai was the most containerised port of India (74.40 per cent of the containerised commodities were being handled by a single port). There has been a considerable decline in the percentage of containerised cargo at the port of Mumbai from 74.40 per cent in 1980–81; 61.65 per cent in 1990–91; 13.54 per cent in 2000–01 to 0.46 per cent in 2011–12. This shift of containerisation is because of a newly developed world-class port of JNPT in the proximity of the Mumbai Port. The JNPT is followed by Chennai, Tuticorin, Kolkata, Cochin, Visakhapatnam and Kandla.

The least containerised ports are Paradip, Murmagao, Mumbai and New Mangalore. The containerisation level of the above ports is less than 1 per cent. The Government must focus on developing better linkages and infrastructure to increase the level of containerisation.

The percentage share of the total traffic trans-shipment is a very small, implying that the Indian ports are really not providing hub services. In terms of port traffic, for every trans-shipment container handled at a hub port, two more handlings would be required—one at the same hub and another at the feeder port. Developing India's container ports to enable direct calls by mainline vessels would provide Indian shippers a better access to the global markets.

The ports in the western region (Mumbai and Gujarat) handle approximately 66 per cent of container throughputs in the country, followed by the ports in the southern region at about 27 per cent and the balance in the eastern region ports. As per literature review, the eastern ports are underleveraged. With specific interventions in terms of terminal-related services and connectivity, the regional balance can move in favour of the eastern ports.

4.10.1 Western Ports' Container Traffic

The ports in the western region (Mumbai and Gujarat clusters) are expected to continue to dominate India's container trades, handling at least two-thirds of the container throughput in the country. This forecast of market share reflects the proximity of the western ports to the major manufacturing and consumption centres in the north-western hinterland, and their access to the extensive container services circulating in the Arabian Sea area. While the regional shares of traffic remain relatively stable, there could be a significant shift in the division of the traffic being handled among the ports in the region.

The JNPT is forecast to remain as India's major container port, but it is expected to face an increasing competition from the ports in the Gujarat region. The private ports of Mundra and Pipavav in Gujarat have already made significant inroads into the container traffic of the north-western hinterland and other Gujarat ports have similar plans. The connectivity issues for the Gujarat ports are being resolved through various innovative public–private partnership arrangements for road and rail connectivity. In Maharashtra, the proposed Rewas-Aware port south of Mumbai, could also create an additional competition for the JNPT. So, the current JNPT/ Mumbai 57 per cent share of the container traffic will likely be eroded as competition in the region increases.

4.10.2 Southern Ports' Container Traffic

The traffic through the southern ports was expected to increase more than four-fold between 2005 and 2015, with a market share of 27 per cent. The NMDP traffic projection for these ports is even more bullish, envisaging the four southern ports of Cochin, Tuticorin, Chennai and Ennore handling 4 mTEUs in 2011–12, or 32 per cent of the total throughput in the Indian ports. The forecasts implicitly assume that the hinterland connectivity of these ports will be improved in a timely manner.

The traffic growth at Cochin will be dependent on the development of the International Container Transshipment Terminal (ICTT) at Vallarpadam. The recent acquisition of the P&O Ports by Dubai Ports World gives the latter control of the ICTT as well as the Colombo Port which is an established trans-shipment terminal with major expansion plans of its own. Developments have also been planned at Tuticorin where the Port of Singapore has the concession for container terminal development. All of these facilities coming on stream should create the conditions for strong competition in the trans-shipment business and provide the shippers with adequate options for efficient container services.

4.10.3 Eastern Ports' Container Traffic

As far as container traffic is concerned, the ports in the east are handicapped by a limited manufacturing base, distance from the main international shipping routes and poor connectivity to the markets and manufacturing centres of northern India. The latter could be corrected with infrastructural improvements but the other two are more difficult constraints. Consequently, the container traffic at the eastern ports shows a limited potential, overall. Among the eastern ports, however, Vishakhapatnam has shown a high growth primarily due to the fast developing state of Andhra Pradesh in its hinterland and its growing consumer economy.

While some eastern ports would appear logical gateways for the containers moving between India and the Far East, it is often more economical to service this trade using the west coast ports which have better access to the mainline container services in the Arabian Sea. Another factor affecting the availability of the direct shipping services from the east coast to the Far East is the systemic imbalance of empty containers heading east from the Gulf countries which results in low freight rates on the exports from India to the Far East. Consequently, east coast ports are expected to continue to rely on feeder services to hubs such as Colombo and Singapore which will allow them to take advantage of this systemic imbalance.

Table 4.2: Level of Containerisation

Readiness Level	*West*	*South*	*East*
High	JNPT, Mundra, Pipavav	Cochin, Chennai	Visakhapatnam
Medium	Kandla, Mumbai	Tuticorin	
Low	New Mangalore, Mormugao	Kolkata, Haldia, Paradip	

Source: Prepared on the basis of NMDP report.

The JNPT handled 4.32 million TEUs of container traffic during the financial year 2011–12 surpassing the previous highest of 4.27 million TEUs during 2010–11, showing a growth of 5.13 per cent from the previous annual container handling of 4.06 million TEUs during the year 2009–10. The container handling at JNPT constitutes about 60 per cent of the total container traffic handled by all the Indian Major Ports which is 7.54 million TEUs.

The share of container traffic in general cargo has been increasing. A substantial part of low volume commodities like electrical and electronic consumer goods, machinery and machinery parts, auto components, iron and steel scrap, newsprint, food products, agriculture products, etc. is amenable to containerisation.

Built in 1983, the Chennai Container Terminal (CCT) is the first container terminal in the Chennai Port. The container terminal was privatised in 2001 and has been operated by the DP World since 30 November 2001 with a capacity of 1.2 million TEUs. The CCT is managed under a 30-year build-operate-transfer agreement set up with the Chennai Port Trust of the Government of India. The terminal is capable of handling fifth generation vessels up to 6,400 TEU and has direct services to China, West Africa, Europe and the United States. It is one of the fastest growing terminals in India with a CAGR of 20 per cent. It has presently four mainline services with a direct connectivity to the Mediterranean countries, Europe, Thailand, Vietnam, China and Korea. The mainline services are complemented by seven weekly feeder services and one coastal service to Colombo, Vishakhapatanam, Penang, Port Klang, Singapore, Yangon and Port Blair, respectively.

Chennai is base to several international carmakers, namely, Ford Motor Co., Hyundai Motor Co., Nissan Motor Co., Renault SA, Daimler AG and BMW AG. Car export (mainly Hyundai) increased by 80.25 per cent to touch 248,697 units during 2008–09 as against 137,971 in the previous year. The Port handled 65 car carriers compared with 40 in the previous year. In 2009, the port shipped nearly 274,000 cars—10 per cent more than the previous year. The Port is now the number one car terminal in the country. After Hyundai, the Port has started attracting global manufacturers like Mahindra, Toyota and Ford. Ford had decided to move exports to the Chennai Port by 2010. Hyundai Motor India is coming up with a first-of-its-kind dedicated automobile terminal at the Chennai Port. The Chennai Port facility is expected to be on the lines of its Ulsan Port, from where it exports half of Korea's 1,500,000 vehicles annually. The company has plans to develop the land into a dedicated terminal to serve as an export base. It is believed that the terminal would basically cater to its export of compact cars from India. The Chennai Port is one of the five major ports in the country that have been identified by the Ministry of

Shipping for the development of cruise terminals—the other four being Goa, Cochin, Mumbai and Mangalore. The Port has had passenger and tourist services to Burma, Malaya, Singapore, Manila, London, Suez, Aden and Colombo for over 100 years. There was also regular passenger traffic during the British rule.

4.11 Containerisation in World and in India: An Overview

In comparison with global containerisation, India is still considerably lagging behind; Shanghai is the premier port followed by Singapore and Hong Kong, respectively. Shenzhen has fourth place in the list of containerisation. In contrast, the JNPT, India's largest container port, was placed at the 30th position. In the list of the top ten containerised ports, China alone has six ports, which portrays the growth dimension of the Chinese economy.

Table 4.3: The World's Top Twenty Container Ports in 2011

Rank	*Port Name*	*Country*	*TEUs (in 000TEUs)*
1	Shanghai	China	31700
2	Singapore	Singapore	29938
3	Hong Kong	China	24384
4	Shenzhen	China	22570
5	Busan	South Korea	16185
6	Ninbo-Zhoushan	China	14686
7	Guangzhou	China	14400
8	Qingdao	China	13020
9	Dubai	UAE	13000
10	Rotterdam	Netherlands	11877
11	Tianjin	China	11500
12	Kaohsiung	Taiwan	9636
13	Port Klang	Malaysia	9604
14	Hamburg	Germany	9022
15	Antwerp	Belgium	8664
16	Los Angeles	USA	7911
17	Tanjung Pelepas	Malaysia	7500
18	Xiamen	China	6461
19	Dalian	China	6400
20	Long Beach	USA	6061

Source: Major Ports of India: A Profile 2011-2012, IPA.

An interesting fact is that the top eight global container terminals (out of ten) are located in Asia and account for more than one-third of the global container traffic. Container traffic has grown at over 10 per cent per annum for the last ten years. This reflects the global dominance of the containerised traffic. About 70 per cent of India's container traffic is trans-shipped though hubs like Colombo, Singapore and Dubai. There has been little action on the Government's plan to set up hub ports to handle container traffic.[9] Privatisation has resulted in a higher supply-led growth. The container volumes of the eastern ports have stagnated; incremental markets are being captured by the western ports.

The container traffic has been shown to exhibit a strong linkage to the GDP growth and most developing countries have demonstrated a high level of correlation between the two. As the economy expands, and manufacturing output and purchasing power increases, imports and exports of the intermediate and finished goods, which are typically containerised, would increase. The trend promises to be a large driver for India's containerised cargo in the future. In addition, the containerisation level in India at 68 per cent is still low compared to the international level of around 80 per cent and an increased penetration of containerisation will also push the traffic volumes and growth rates. The container demand was forecast to grow from the current 6.5 million TEUs in 2008–09 to about 21 million TEUs by 2015. As regards to the combined traffic of thermal and coking coal, India presently imports about 8 per cent of its coal consumption of about 370 million tonnes; however, port traffic also includes the coastal movement of domestic thermal coal from the east coast to the west coast ports. Presently, over 75 per cent of the coal traffic is concentrated along the east coast as a result of the location of both the mining centres and the steel-making capacity in the east. The thermal coal traffic at India's major ports grew to 43.4 million tonnes in 2009–10. The power sector consumes two-third of the domestic production, with the remainder being for the steel and cement industries. The large power generation capacity enhancements proposed will drive a growing level of coal imports and coastal movements. The thermal coal traffic at the ports was slated to increase by more than two-and-a-half times by 2015 and much of the increase was expected in the western region ports due to an expected expansion in the power sector demand there. Coking coal imports grew at almost 16 per cent per annum and reached to a level of 27.1 million tonnes by 2008–09 at Major Ports. Imports of coking coal were expected to more than double to 53 million tonnes by 2015, reflecting a growing domestic supply. The east coast ports are expected to handle over 75 per cent of the future imports with the ports in Orissa and Andhra Pradesh, barring Krishnapatnam, accounting for much of the traffic owing to the steel-making capacity being largely located in this region.

Containers offer the advantages of being cheap, fast, regular and reliable. Worldwide, the container fleets have increased at an extraordinary rate. With the advent of containerisation, several of the efficiency parameters of the Indian ports have improved dramatically. At present, the average turnaround time for the ships has reduced from over four days in the late 1990s to 1–2 days or even less than a day. Average berthing delays have also reduced to less than half of the previous levels. Of the 12 Major Ports of India, the JNPT and the Mumbai Port Trust have been the frontrunners in the creation of container capacity with a combined market share of more than 57 per cent of the total container traffic. Other ports have lagged behind due to a lack of adequate infrastructure in the form of container-handling equipment, container freight station networks and rail networks.

The JNPT's own terminal, JNPCT, increased its throughput by 19.72 per cent over the last year in terms of tonnage and 17.3 per cent in terms of TEUs. The NSICT's throughput fell by 8.8 per cent in terms of the TEUs as compared to last year. The total traffic of 65.75 million tonnes and container traffic of 4.32 million TEUs have been highest since the inception of the Port. The JNP Container Terminal crossed more than 1 million TEUs/14.53 million tonnes—a growth of 19.72 per cent year-on-year. The container traffic of 1.89 million TEUs handled at the APM Terminals, Mumbai, has also been the highest since the inception of the terminal. The previous highest was 1.86 million TEUs in 2010–11.

The factors driving the future traffic demand in the various port clusters are (i) regional economic growth and creation of new manufacturing sites

(ii) improvements in port connectivity that make specific ports more accessible (iii) changes in Indian and global shipping patterns that impact the routing decisions of Indian shippers and (iv) actions by local governments and port managers to increase the port's reach in the country's container trade. The first two drivers can be modelled and their impact on the future traffic volumes estimated. The third driver can also be modelled, though with less precision as it is a daunting task to predict how the future global shipping patterns will evolve and impact the shippers' routing decisions. The fourth driver is dependent on the decisions at the local level that create a competitive edge and determine who gains or loses the market share. The last is the focus of a strategy development and business planning activity now being undertaken by each of the Major Ports at the urging of the Planning Commission and the National Development Council.

NOTES

1 http://www.sagarsandesh.com/news/containerization-challenges.
2 National Conference on Container Infrastructure in India 2012, Background Paper. (http://www.deloitte.com/assets/DcomIndia/Local%20Assets/Documents/Thoughtware/Containerization%20Infrastructure%20in%20India%201402_Final.pdf)
3 G. Raghuram and Rachna Gangwar, Indian Institute of Management Ahmedabad, August 2007.
4 *Business Line*, January 28, 2004.
5 Ibid.
6 World Bank, Report 2007.
7 World Bank, Report 2007.
8 Ibid.
9 Basic Port Statistics of India (2002-03), MOST, GOI, p.12.

5

Governance in the Port System

The Major Ports are under the purview of the Central Government, while the other ports (minor and intermediate ports) come under the jurisdiction of their respective State Governments.[1] The states with Maritime Boards are Gujarat, Maharashtra and Tamil Nadu while the states without Maritime Boards are Kerala, Andhra Pradesh, Goa, Karnataka, Orissa and West Bengal; the Union Territories also do not have Maritime Boards.[2] Currently, the Port Sector is governed by a plethora of complex laws and regulations. These include the Indian Ports Act (1908), the Inland Vessels Act (1838), the Dock Workers (Regulation of Employment) Act (1948), the Merchant Shipping Act (1958), the Major Port Trusts Act (1963), and the Dock Workers (Safety, Health and Welfare) Act (1986).[2] The Port Sector lacks an independent, full-fledged regulatory authority. At present, regulation is done through the Tariff Authority of Major Ports (TAMP), which was formed in March 1997. Ennore is an exception here because it does not come under its jurisdiction.[3] Its functions are threefold—namely, the regulation of the tariffs levied by the major port trusts and the private terminals therein; fixing rates for the services rendered as well as for the use of properties and setting the governing conditions that influence the application of the rates. Overall, the TAMP aims to use tariffs to bring about operational efficiency, to rationalise tariffs and to systematise the tariff-setting systems across all the Major Ports. But, the financial institutions want these things consolidated into a single law for better performance and efficiency.[4]

5.1 The Structure of the Ports in India

The classification of the Indian ports into major, minor and intermediate has an administrative significance. The Indian government has a federal structure, and according to the Constitution, maritime transport falls under the "Concurrent List", to be administered by both the Central and the State governments.[5] While the Central Shipping Ministry administers the Major Ports, the minor and intermediate ports are administered by the relevant departments or ministries in the nine coastal states—namely, West Bengal, Orissa, AndhraPradesh, Tamilnadu, Kerala, Karnataka, Goa, Maharashtra and Gujarat. Several of these 189 minor and intermediate ports have been merely "notified"; little or no cargo handling actually takes place. These ports have been identified by the respective governments to be developed in a phased manner; a good proportion involving a public–private partnership.[6]

The Government of India administers all the important Indian ports of the country mentioned in the Union List of the Indian Constitution under the Indian Ports Act, 1908 and the Major Port Trust Act, 1963.[7] The Government of India nominates a Board of Trustees which is comprised of responsible persons from the government departments and public enterprises who are given the authority to look after each Major Port. These Board members have little independent power and have to follow the policy matters and orders from the Government of India for the ports' administrative issues.[8]

The Major Ports are under the Union List, while the Non-Major Ports are under the Concurrent List of the Constitution of India. The 12 Major Ports are administered by the Central Government under the Ministry of Shipping. The remaining ports which are referred to as Non-Major Ports are administered by the nine maritime states and the three Union Territories within their respective coastlines.[9]

In order to achieve the coveted goal of transforming the Indian ports into world-class facilities suited to the requirements of the future economy of India, the Ministry of Shipping, Government of India, has initiated many path-breaking measures which will facilitate an enhanced private investment, improve the service quality and promote competitiveness, apart from achieving the expansion of capacities in the country. Such measures include the formulation of a Maritime Policy, revision of various operational policies, preparation of Perspective Plans for the major ports, commissioning of two more major ports—one each for the eastern and western coasts—introduction of the Port Community System (PCS), paperless regime, etc.[10]

In the year 2010, as decided in the meeting of the Committee of Infrastructure headed by the Honourable Prime Minister, the major ports were asked to prepare a long prospective business plan of each port with the help of international consultants. Accordingly, each major port has got its business plans prepared. All those plans have been coordinated at the Central level by the Indian Ports Association, New Delhi, by engaging the Port of Rotterdam Authority. A consolidated business plan, combining the projections of traffic and development plans, was also prepared. But, such a consolidated plan is only for the Major Ports and does not take into consideration the needs of the Non-Major Ports which are large in number irrespective of their volumes. The now defunct Planning Commission also, in its mid-term appraisal document, had strongly suggested having a comprehensive document for the development of the Port Sector that included the Non-Major Ports, and also a monitoring system for assessing the overall port capacities, including those of the Non-Major Ports, on a regular basis[11]. It is in this context that the Ministry of Shipping embarked upon the very challenging task of preparing an ambitious Maritime Agenda, 2010–2020, in order to create, build and sustain the maritime infrastructural needs of the country for the next decade.

The maritime sector comprises Ports, Merchant Shipping, Ship Building/Ship Repair and Inland Water Transport. The capacity expansion in the Port Sector is being taken up through several development activities—namely, construction/upgradation of berths, deepening of channels, rail/road connectivity projects, equipment upgradation/modernisation schemes and other related schemes for the creation of backup facilities. The objective is to upgrade and modernise the port infrastructure in India which will enable it to benchmark its performance as against global standards.[12]

With the opening up of the Indian economy, the Government of India has allowed private sector participation in the Major Ports for infusing funds, inducting the latest technology, improved management practices and above all, the addition of capacity. A foreign direct investment up to 100 per cent has been permitted for the construction and maintenance of the ports and harbours. To encourage private sector participation, the Ministry of Shipping has already put in place the guidelines for private sector participation. Having set the tone for the growth path, the Indian Major Ports and Non-Major Ports have formulated ambitious plans for the development of new outlets, augmentation of existing service centres, induction of state-of-art cargo-handling equipment and improvement in logistics in order to meet the challenges emanating from the anticipated growth in trade.[13]

In addition to capacity augmentation, all the Major Ports are aiming at bringing structural changes in the administration of the ports to improve organisational effectiveness. To this end, all the ports are planning towards implementing the 'Landlord Port' concept, duly limiting their role to the maintenance of channels and basic infrastructure and leaving the development and operational management of the terminal and cargo-handling facilities to the private sector. The ports are aiming at a lean staff by extending information technology to the entire gamut of operations. Thus, the Indian ports are marching forward at a confident note and gearing themselves to meet the anticipated demand from trade in the years to come.

While the present policies in the Government—both Central and State—are quite dynamic and investor-friendly, it is imperative that some more path-breaking initiatives be taken over a period of time in order to boost the sector to the huge anticipated levels of growth and development of the ports in terms of traffic as well as capacity. It would also be necessary to review the policies periodically—say once in three years—to keep them relevant to the changing times.

Figure 5.1: Structure of the Proposed Model for Privatisation of the Major Ports Through Corporatisation

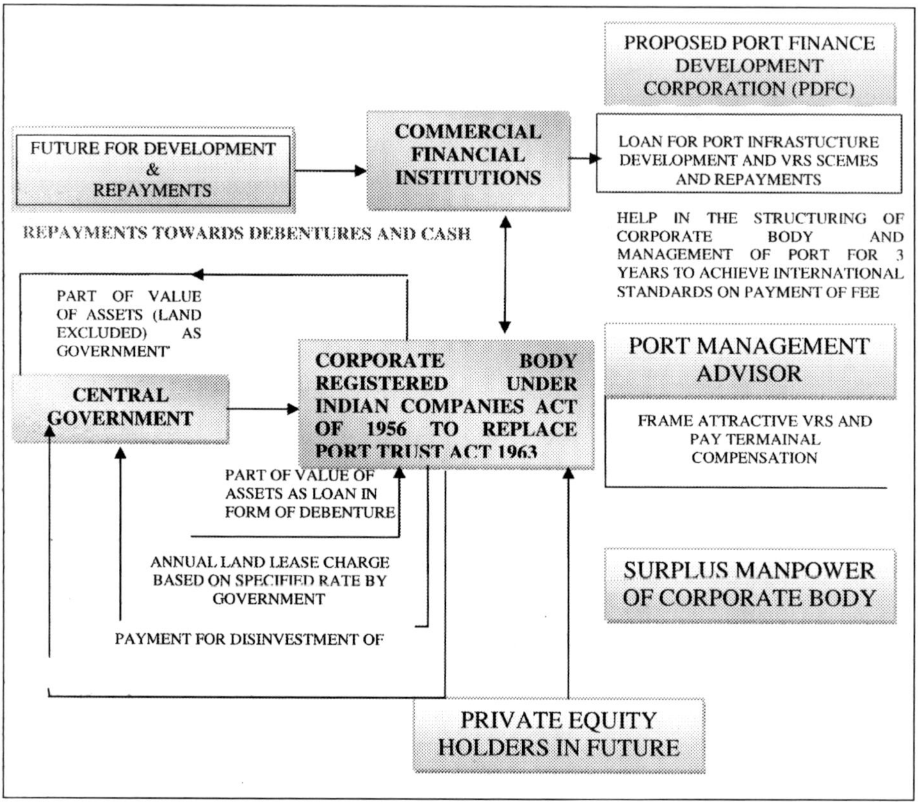

Source: Prepared on the Basis of a Perspective Plan for Indian Port Sector Vision 2020, Vol. II, Apr. 2001, Rites Ltd.

5.2 The Model of the 'Landlord Port'

The 'Landlord Port' is characterised by its mixed public–private orientation. Under this model, the port authority acts as a regulatory body and as a landlord, while the port operations (especially cargo handling) are carried out by the private companies. Today, the 'Landlord Port' is the dominant port model in the larger and medium-sized ports.[14] There are more than 2,000 seaports active throughout the world for catering to the requirements of seaborne cargo. With the growing move for the privatisation of the seaports all over the world subsequent to reforms, the private sector participation in the operations and infrastructural activities of the seaports has increased substantially over the last few years. This has resulted in a radical change in the organisational model of the ports, converting them from a 'Service Port' model to the 'Landlord Port' model, wherein the port authority retains the port's infrastructure and regulatory functions, whereas the port services are provided by the private operators.[15]

The port authority constitutes a landlord, which manages the basic port assets by lending land and infrastructure to the port operators in an efficient manner. The Landlord Port in this model would be involved in the planning, lease negotiation, safety, navigation and overall coordinating functions.[16] Cargo services, marine service, ancillary services, berths, etc., are privatised on a captive/BOT basis for the primary port users. The port operators as well as the undertakings which need to be located in the port, lease the land, the infrastructure and the associated services and provide them to the secondary users—cargo owners, ship owners and cargo-ship owners.[17]

5.2.1 Major Ports to be Landlord Ports

The Major Ports have been working towards implementing the Landlord Port concept; this approach will continue and a total realisation of this concept is expected by 2020.

5.3 Policy on PPP Projects

Public–Private Partnerships will be the preferred mode for the development of port terminals and other commercially viable activities in the Major Ports.

5.4 Land Policy

The land policy is one of the significant policy frameworks guiding the overall functioning of the Port Sector. In all the major ports the world over, land has been leveraged for optimising the throughput and increasing the revenue of the ports. It is an established practice globally for the ports to allot land for carrying out economic activity, including establishing industry, to ensure a captive cargo to the port, thereby enhancing the sustainability of that port. Port land has also been used to set up Special

Economic Zones (SEZs) aimed at encouraging industrial development in and around that port.[18] Other than the above, ports are generally expected to utilise their land giving first priority to the purpose of port-related activities and treating the activities incidental to the port as secondary in nature. Ports located in large cities present the port planners with special challenges in land management. Major city-ports offer opportunities for the economic development of their host cities in terms of the utilisation of land. Keeping all these factors in view, the land policy should be reviewed from time to time and a new vibrant land policy put in place, in tune with the times.[19]

5.5 The Policy for Preventing Monopoly in the Major Ports Sector

In terms of the Regulatory Framework of the Private Sector Participation (PSP) Guidelines (1996), the ports were directed to ensure that a private investment does not result in the creation of private monopolies and that private facilities are available to all the users on equal and competitive terms.[20] Accordingly, it was felt that a policy may be formulated for the prevention of a private monopoly in the Port Sector for ensuring a healthy competition amongst the private operators and a smooth award of projects for capacity augmentation at the Major Ports. In exercise of the powers conferred upon the Central Government under Section 111 of the Major Port Trusts Act, 1963 and in consultation with the Chairpersons of all the Major Ports as well as the stakeholders, the following policy has been laid down with effect from 2 August 2010 for preventing a private sector monopoly in the Major Ports:[21] If there is only one private terminal/berth operator in a port for a specific cargo, the operator of that berth or his associates shall not be allowed to bid for the next terminal/berth for handling the same cargo in the same port.

5.6 Corporatisation of the Major Ports and Commercialisation

There are 12 Ports directly under the Central Government and of these, 11 Major Ports are governed by the Major Port Trusts Act, 1963, and one (Ennore Port Limited) was incorporated as a company under the

Companies Act, 1956 and is governed by the Indian Ports Act, 1908. Corporatisation envisages the conversion of the Major Ports into commercial organisations operating with minimum costs, offering improved services and having a quick market-oriented commercial response mechanism. Towards this end, the corporatisation of ports has been recommended by experts and will be achieved in phases. Corporatisation will be taken up for three ports in the first phase, beginning with the JNPT.[22] The deserving ports could be conferred with a Navaratna or Miniratna status, giving them substantial autonomy in functioning. Public ports under the control of both the Central Government and the State Governments should completely retune themselves and focus on commercialisation and corporatisation, with professional management in place and free access to financial markets without any recourse to government support.

5.7 Tariff Regulation at the Major Ports

TAMP is the economic regulator for the Major Ports with the key function being tariff determination for the Major Ports and their private terminals. TAMP was established in 1997 by an amendment to the Major Port Trusts Act, 1963 with the key objective of determining tariffs for the Major Ports and also specifying the conditions governing these tariffs. TAMP follows a normative cost-based approach which recognises the capital and operating costs and allows a reasonable rate of return on the capital deployed—which is 16 per cent as of now—based on a capacity utilisation of 70 per cent of the capital deployed.[23]

5.8 Port Regulator

While the Tariff Authority of the Major Ports is the economic regulator for the Major Ports, with the main function being tariff-setting for the Major Ports and the private terminals commissioned therein, the Non-Major Ports, operating in the same environment do not have any economic regulator and they, including the private ports, have the liberty to fix their own tariffs. As a result, there is no level playing field.[24] Hence, there is a need for a Port Regulator for all the ports for setting, monitoring and regulating the service levels, technical and performance standards. All the ports should be left free to fix their tariff, depending upon the interplay of the market forces. The Regulator can be entrusted with the responsibility of dispute resolution as appropriate. The Regulator may also be empowered with judicial powers to issue regulations and policy guidelines, and take specific regulatory actions upon the finding of an inadequate competition, anti-competitive practices or unsafe or environmentally detrimental practices. The Regulator could also act as an Ombudsman to deal with the consumer grievances.

5.9 Environmental Clearance Mechanism

India is in the process of creating a huge capacity through the Public–Private Partnership basis. One of the major factors for the delay in the fructification of projects is the long environmental clearance mechanism. The project authorities have to undergo different processes at the State and Central levels to get the project environmentally cleared. It is in the interest of the Port Sector that the environmental clearance process be reviewed in respect of the existing ports where further development works are being undertaken. It should be possible to have clear guidelines laid down by the Environment Ministry and leave it to the administrative agencies/state Government to comply with those guidelines strictly and clear the projects environmentally. A Master Plan for the entire port, covering different projects, may be prepared and in-principle clearance be taken from the Environment Ministry and thereafter, a specific clearance for each project may be obtained from the administrative agency/state government. These could also be subject to a subsequent environmental audit. It would also be desirable to look at the global best practices for environmental clearance.[25]

5.10 Environment Policy and Green Ports

The Ministry of Shipping is committed to the protection of the environment, as it is an indispensable factor for sustainable economic growth. Steps are to be taken by the ports in their endeavour to become clean, green and environment-friendly. Environmental issues including the handling of hazardous and noxious substances in a port, prevention of air, water and soil pollution, the treatment of harmful aquatic organisms in the ballast water etc., are being addressed and tackled.[26] The port industry in general has been faced with sustainability issues and compliance to the international and national regulations vis-à-vis the demands for a bigger port capacity and increased productivity without compromising upon the environmental quality. Without regulation, it is difficult to implement greener practices, as these may put the operators at a competitive disadvantage. In addition to the need for increased regulation, there are several other issues that are appearing across the marine and port sector. These include the availability of incentives for encouraging green practices, the cost and availability of clean fuel, the need to do more research on green technologies, the use of shoreside power, the training programmes for such industry and in designating the emission control areas.[27]

Hence, more emphasis is to be given on the use of cleaner fuel and the technology leading to an improvement in the air quality and public health. There is a need to develop green policies supported by the incentives to encourage ports for implementing green practices. The Jawaharlal Nehru Port Trust has already taken a lead in this regard. Green practices in the marine and port sector would need a collaboration with the other sectors (air quality concerns, etc).

5.11 Capacity Building and Human Resource Development

Recognising the need to impart a structured training to all the port personnel including officers, it is essential to retrain them in multi-skilling. Every employee should undergo different tiers of the training programme during his service.

5.11.1 Indian Maritime Cadre

The maritime sector is a specialised sector and the decisions in most of its areas are driven by the experience of the executives in the sector, who through their professional experience and expertise, can contribute to its growth and development. It should be possible to have several key positions in the sector manned by maritime specialists. In addition, the executives in the sector do not have any proper career progression plans. As a result, they lack motivation and are unable to contribute their mite to the sector in spite of their specialisation. Hence, there is a need to form an Indian Maritime Cadre and encourage specialisation in this field.[28]

5.11.2 Pilots Pool

The Indian ports suffer, many-a-time, from an inadequacy of pilots to navigate the vessels in their channels. As a result, the ports are unable to achieve a zero pre-detention time for vessels and a long waiting time of the vessels is also common.

5.12 Dredging

The ports need to develop the capacity to receive bigger ships, for which capital dredging to achieve the desired level of draft and maintenance dredging to retain that level have to be undertaken. In most of the maritime nations, dredging in the channels, both capital as well as maintenance, is taken up with budgetary support from either the national government or the local governments.

Financial support for dredging is necessary for reducing the port charges. The channels leading to the Major Ports could be declared as National or State Channels. If considered necessary, each port may be asked to remit a certain Dredging Contribution to the concerned Government in proportion of the quantum of traffic handled by that port.[29]

5.13 Rail–Road Connectivity

Although the Major Ports have a reasonably adequate rail–road connectivity, many Non-Major Ports are suffering from severe constraints. Such ports must work with the State Governments and other authorities to commission a 4-lane road connectivity and a 2-lanes rail connectivity at their ports so as to ensure a seamless flow of cargo. The Major Ports may endeavour, in consultation with the National Highways Authority of India (NHAI) and the Ministry of Railways, to expand their connectivity to 8-lane road connectivity and a 4-lane rail-connectivity, respectively, by 2020. Links with the Western Dedicated Freight Corridor and the Eastern Freight

Corridor are a must for the Indian ports to live up to the challenges of burgeoning trade and must be pursued to be in place at the earliest.[30]

5.14 Hub Ports

India should commission at least four hub ports—two on the east viz. Chennai and Visakhapatnam and two on the west coast viz. the Jawaharlal Nehru Port and Cochin, in order to receive the 13,500 TEU containerships.[31]

5.15 Tax Regime

Since the beginning, the Major Ports in this country have been treated as local authority by virtue of a provision in the General Clauses Act and they have been exempted from the Income Tax as ports are considered as a nation's vital infrastructure and the surpluses generated in the ports could be ploughed back for the creation of more infrastructures both within and outside the port. Similar had been the case with the State Maritime Boards also. However, during the year 2002, the Income Tax Act was amended to tax the ports also. The taxation system must also promote investments in the infrastructure.[32]

5.16 Cruise Shipping

India being a major tourist destination, Cruise Shipping is an area which has a vast potential for the Indian ports. Though a policy has been formulated, Cruise Shipping has not really taken off as it should have. A comprehensive policy needs to be evolved and adequate arrangements in terms of the state-of-the-art passenger terminals, baggage screening, customs clearance, immigration, tourism-related ancillaries backed up by effective publicity need to be in place so that the Indian ports also become truly world-class destinations as in the cases of Singapore, Dubai and several west European and Caribbean countries.

5.17 Indian Maritime Finance Corporation

Most of the maritime projects are specialised in nature and they require a specialised scrutiny and appraisal for obtaining the finances for such projects. Moreover, there are no specialised agencies to fund such projects. As a result, many-a-time, project authorities in the maritime sector find it difficult to raise finances and achieve financial closure. Many ports possess considerable cash reserves which, in order to be utilised for expansion and developmental activities, are deposited in banks because of the induction of the PPP in this sector. These deposits yield low returns. On the other hand, a good maritime project, if appraised properly, might yield very good returns. Hence, it is quite desirable to float a specialised Maritime Finance Corporation with an equity of the ports and financial institutions for funding the port projects.[33]

5.18 Corporate Social Responsibility

Corporate social responsibility encompasses the sectors like health, education, employment, income and the quality of life. It should be binding on the corporate sector to work on the above aspects, which are thought to be primary social indicators. The concept of Corporate Social Responsibility (CSR) has so far failed to take deep roots in India.[34] Much needs to be done to bring a change in the attitude towards the CSR and bring awareness among the corporates about their social responsibilities. The Department of Public Enterprises (DPE) has prepared guidelines for the central public sector enterprises to take up important corporate social responsibility projects to be funded by a 2–5 per cent of the company's net profits. Nearly all the Major Ports in India are involved in CSR programmes in the areas like education, health, staff quarters, skill development and training. The Major Ports are also promoting encouragement to the outstanding children of the port employees through scholarships, etc.[35]

5.19 Approaches to International Cooperation

To widen the port's horizon, a continuous coordination and cooperation is to be maintained with international organisations like the *International Association of Ports and Harbours* (IAPH) (of which most of the ports are members), the World Association for Waterborne Transport Infrastructure, World Bank, European Union, the *Economic and Social Commission for Asia and the Pacific* (ESCAP), the *United Nations Conference on Trade and*

Development (UNCTAD), the *Asian Development Bank* (*ADB*), etc.[36] In fact, the ports are aligned with the *International Maritime Organization* (IMO) and the International Convention for the *Safety of Life at Sea* (*SOLAS*) Convention documents for the safe and secure handling of various type of cargo. Most of the leading ports have already implemented the International Ship and Port Facility Security (*ISPS*) code. Though a number of Major Ports have established sister-port agreements with some of the world-class ports, there is a further need to strengthen such cooperation for sharing the expertise in cargo-handling operations and port management, exchange of information, cooperation in training needs and module development, establishing joint ventures of mutual interest, promoting synergy and trade facilitation in the areas of their expertise, etc. The sister-port arrangements may cover bilateral financial and technical cooperation through an exchange of technology relating to infrastructural development and environment, management and operations, collaborations on dredging, marketing of port services, etc.[37]

5.20 Competition and Cooperation among Ports

In the era of globalisation where the economy grows at a brisk pace, every industry is witnessing competition between the many players. The Port Sector is no exception. The inter-port competition as well as intra-port competition is quite evident in the recent times. In India, inter-port competition is hindered mostly by insufficient hinterland connectivity. Further, there are rigidities in pricing as a result of which the traffic of the nearby ports cannot be enticed by value-added services or reduction in tariff. These issues need to be resolved in order to promote inter-port competition in an efficient market. One can expect more competition to emerge; once more ports are developed by the private operators in the bigger maritime states. The Central Government has taken a decision of not allowing a particular player to dominate a port; this should promote an intra-port competition in future. With the emergence of new ports and terminals lined up in the future, there is a need of a government policy for meeting these competitive challenges.[38]

While competition is very vital for the growth and development of industry as well as to ensure a quality of service to trade at competitive prices, at times, there are situations where cooperation among the competing players also becomes essential. There is a need to practice business ethics as well as to avoid unfair practices for which cooperation among all the relevant players is essential. There are certain circumstances wherein cooperation among the different terminals or ports becomes necessary in operational exigencies as well as in emergency situations. Similarly, in case of illegal strikes taking place at a terminal, creating a difficult situation to the management and trade, the other terminals should come forward and rescue the terminal in difficulty, by handling their cargo at the usual tariff. The same broad principle of cooperation should be adopted by the all the ports in the country to see that the Indian cargo does not get diverted to the neighbouring countries. Of course, a usual competition based on efficiency, productivity, cost effectiveness and marketing must continue and thrive in the ports and terminals.[39]

5.21 Legislative Framework

The Governments, both Central and State, should transform the legislative framework in tune with the current requirements. Necessary amendments to the Major Ports Act, 1963, the Indian Ports Act, 1908 and the Maritime Board Acts of respective state governments have to be carried out.[40]

5.22 The Indian Ports: A Global Perspective

In the era of globalisation, infrastructural sectors all over the world have gone global in the form of acquisitions, equity stakes in the companies abroad, commissioning of greenfield projects, partnering with the companies abroad by way of joint ventures etc.; the Port sector is no exception. The Port of Singapore Authority has established its wings in the different part of the world by an instrument called PSA International. Similarly, the Dubai Port too has spread its wings internationally by the consolidated company viz. DP World. Likewise, some ports in Europe too have made their presence in the rest of the world.[41] It has been felt in this context that since India is bestowed with a rich maritime heritage and immense expertise in operating ports with a highly skilled manpower and specialised knowledge in the port operations, it must also float a special purpose vehicle for making investments in the ports abroad and become a truly global power in the Port Sector worldwide.[42]

5.22.1 *Port Capacity*

1. Major ports to provide draft of not less than 14 metres and for hub ports, 17 metres
2. Full mechanisation of cargo handling and movement in the Major Ports
3. Development of adequate storage areas in the Major Ports
4. Identification and implementation of projects for rail, road and inland waterway connectivity to the Ports
5. Development of two hub ports each on the western and the eastern coasts: Mumbai (JNPT), Cochin, Chennai and Visakhapatnam
6. Encouraging the Major Ports to set up ship repair and maintenance hubs

5.22.2 *Port Policy Measures*

1. Corporatisation of Major Ports
2. Major Ports to be landlord ports
3. Periodic review of the processes and documents for PPP
4. A new land policy for the Major Ports
5. A new policy for captive berths in the Major Ports
6. Establishing a Port Regulator for all the ports for setting, monitoring and regulating the service levels and the technical and performance standards
7. Proposing simplification of the environment clearance process
8. A policy on cooperation and competition among the Indian ports
9. Establishment of 'Indian Ports Global' for overseas investments by the Indian Ports
10. Ports to work towards being 'green ports'

5.22.3 *Technology for Efficiency, Safety and Security*

1. Ports to use information technology for quality performance

2. Port Community system to be fully integrated with all the stakeholders
3. Introduction of modern security systems in the ports
4. Completion and operationalisation of the VTS in the Gulf of Kutch

5.22.4 Environment

1. Ports to work towards being 'green ports'
2. Designation of an Emission Control Area (ECA) for specific portions of the Indian coastal waters
3. Marine disaster and oil pollution response mechanism
4. Use of non-conventional sources of energy for the lighthouses and the aids to navigation
5. Promotion of the building of 'green ships'

5.22.5 Human Resources

1. Human Resources Development in shipping
2. Additional campuses for the Indian Maritime University (IMU) in the major coastal cities
3. New courses in specialised areas in Engineering, Management, Law, etc. in the IMU campuses
4. Collaboration of the IMU with top global academic institutions in the maritime sector
5. Creation of additional facilities and improvement of seamen's hostels
6. Capacity building for port personnel
7. Pilot training
8. Improving port-based facilities for seafarers
9. Centres in shipbuilding education and training to promote the skills in shipbuilding
10. Enhance capabilities for ship design
11. State-level Inland Waterways Crew Training Centres in close interaction with NINI, Patna;
12. Promotion of research in various areas in the maritime sector

5.22.6 *Shipping Policy*

(i) Increase Indian tonnage through necessary policy interventions
(ii) Declaration of a new coastal shipping policy
(iii) Promoting river–sea vessels
(iv) Financial incentives
(v) Infrastructural facilities
(vi) Legal issues
(vii) Database and communication infrastructure
(viii) Cabotage policy support
(ix) Customs processes and procedures
(x) Policy on cargo support
(xi) Establishment of a 'Freight Exchange'
(xii) Creation of Ombudsman/Tribunals for shipping matters
(xiii) Formation of an independent Marine Casualty Investigation Cell

5.22.7 *Finance*

1. A Maritime Finance Corporation
2. Study of Taxation Systems
3. Tonnage Tax
4. Income Tax for the ports
5. Income Tax for the seafarers
6. Customs duties on bunkers and repair materials

5.22.8 *Shipping Programmes*

1. SCI to have ambitious vessel acquisition plans to lead the growth in Indian tonnage
2. SCI to increase container-handling capacity
3. Introduction of passenger ferry services between India and Sri Lanka
4. Introduction of passenger ferry services between India and Maldives
5. Introduction of passenger ferry services between India and other nearby countries

6. Introduction of coastal ferry-cum-passenger services for Chennai to Kanyakumari, and other suitable places
7. Introduction of faster vessels to Lakshadweep
8. Strengthening the Navigational Safety in Ports Committee (NSPC)
9. Strengthening of capacity for Port State Control and Flag State Inspections
10. Promotion of multimodal transport operations for door to door delivery

5.22.9 Shipbuilding and Repairs

1. Grant of Infrastructure Status to shipbuilding industry
2. A scheme for capital subsidy for encouraging adoption of world-class technologies by the Indian shipbuilding industry
3. Expansion and modernisation of shipyards
4. Promotion of the building of 'green ships'
5. Formulation of a policy to promote/facilitate maritime clusters including shipbuilding and ship repair hubs and ship ancillary units
6. Centres in shipbuilding education and training to promote the skills in shipbuilding
7. Enhance capabilities for ship design
8. Liberalisation of the scheme for registration of ship repair units.

5.22.10 Inland Waterways

1. Development of IWT infrastructure
2. Reliable fairway with an assured least available depth for round-the-year and round-the-clock navigation
3. Terminals for the berthing of vessels and an interface with road and rail
4. Quantum jump in public funding in IWT sector
5. Declaration of River Barak as National Waterway No. 6
6. Development of the National Waterways 4 and 5
7. Development of stretches of the National Waterways through the PPP mode

8. Extension of National Waterway No. 3 in Kerala
9. States, especially the North-East states, to develop feeder routes to the National Waterways or major waterways

5.22.11 Institutional Development

1. Formation of an Indian Maritime Council to bring together all sectors of maritime activities, both public and private
2. Creation of a Shipping Sectoral Innovation Council
3. Promotion of research in various areas in the maritime sector
4. A Maritime Finance Corporation

5.22.12 Legislation

1. Enactment of a new Indian Ports Act replacing the Indian Ports Act, 1908 and the Major Port Trusts Act, 1963;

5.22.13 International Matters

1. Control of piracy through concerted international actions
2. Bilateral maritime agreements with selected countries/regions for mutual benefit
3. A framework for cooperation between the Indian ports and those in other countries
4. Establishment of 'Indian Ports Global' for overseas investments by Indian Ports

5.22.14 General

1. Establishment of State Maritime Boards in all the coastal states

The Indian Port Sector has been broadly divided into two broad categories: Major Ports and Non-Major Ports. The latter is commonly referred to as 'minor' and 'intermediate' ports. The legal distinction between the major and minor ports is made on the Constitutional principle of the sharing of resources and revenues between the Central and State Governments. This technical nomenclature is also based on the legal distinctions made under the two key source laws that govern the port sector in the country, viz. the Indian Ports Act, 1908 and the Major Port Trusts Act, 1963. More specifically, the definition of 'major' and 'minor' and

Figure 5.2: Major Steps in Corporatisation and Privatisation of a Major Port

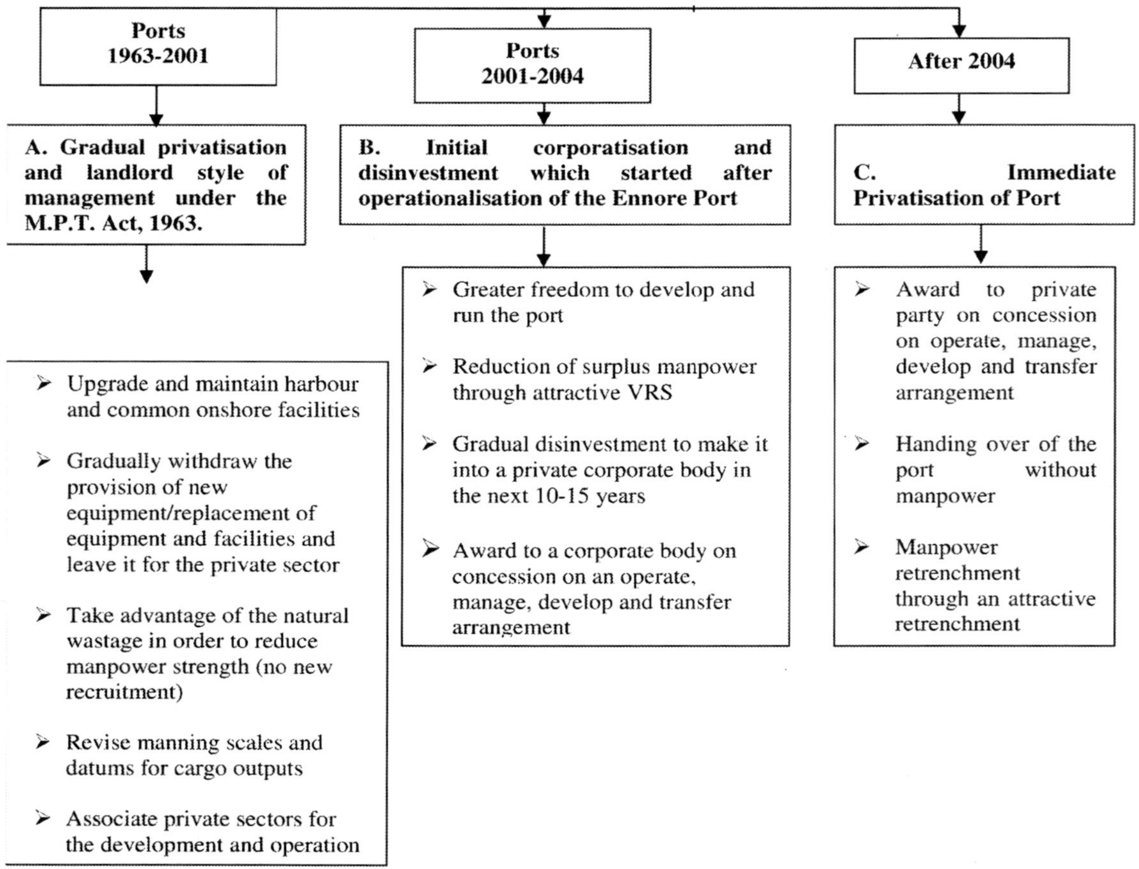

Source: Prepared on the Basis of Perspective Plan for Indian Port Sector Vision 2020, Vol.II, Apr. 2001, Rites Ltd.

'intermediate' ports in India is based on the list of central, concurrent and state subjects, as listed under the Indian Constitution.[43] The Major Ports are administered under the Major Port Trusts Act of 1963 and fall under the direct jurisdiction of the Central Government. The Ministry in charge of the ports is the Ministry of Shipping (earlier called the Ministry of Surface Transport—MOST). These ports are governed and managed by the Port Trusts which are administered by a Board of Trustees covering a wide representation comprising of elected members of the legislature and Parliament, government officials, labour representatives and industry representatives.[44]

5.23 Management of the Minor Ports

Pursuant to the Indian Ports Act, 1908, the responsibility for the development of the Minor Ports in the maritime states of India vests with the concerned State Government. No permission is required from the Central Government to establish a Minor Port. They are placed in the Concurrent List of the Constitution and are administered under the Indian Ports Act, 1908. The nine maritime states control some 189 state ports and jetties, of which more than sixty are truly operational. At the state level, the State Maritime Boards are responsible for the formulation of waterfront development policies and plans, regulating and overseeing the management of Minor Ports, attracting private investment in the development of such ports, enforcing environmental protection standards, etc.[45]

For the maritime states, the Maritime Boards have become the dominant public port management model. The Maritime Boards have their legal basis in various State Acts such as the Gujarat Maritime Board Act, 1981 (the first Maritime Board in India) and the Tamil Nadu Maritime Board Act, 1995. The Maritime Boards are in charge of all the Minor Ports in their state; they administer, control, regulate and manage them.

The typical tasks of a Maritime Board are as follows[46]:

1. Framing of rules for the administration and operation of ports
2. To levy port dues and other charges
3. To provide the necessary infrastructural facilities for the landing

and shipping of cargoes, etc. and to maintain an adequate depth in the channel for safe navigation

4. Declaration of port limits and landing places at the ports
5. Rendering pilotage services
6. Detaining un-seaworthy ships
7. Issuing Certificate of Entry and Clearance
8. Affording assistance for communication between shore and ship with Very High Frequency (VHF)/Morse/Flag Signals
9. Rendering assistance to the vessels in distress;
10. Conducting preliminary enquiries into wrecks and casualties
11. Issuing pilot licences for private pilotage at the Minor Ports

5.24 Maritime States Development Council

The Maritime States Development Council (MSDC) was constituted in May 1997 under the chairmanship of the Minister of Shipping to have an integrated approach for the development of both the Major Ports and Non-Major Ports.[47] The Ministers in charge of Ports in all the maritime states, the Union Territories of Pondicherry, Andaman and Nicobar Administration, Daman and Diu and the Lakshadweep Islands are its members. The deliberations and decisions of the MSDC provide the institutional framework for a coordinated development of the Major Ports and Non-Major Ports.[48]

NOTES

1 R. Ramakrishanan (2003), "Scenario of Port Handling and Vision", *Indian Ports*, Vol. 35(2), Oct., pp.5-17.
2 "Port Financing: Still a Trickle", *Indian Infrastructure*, July 2001, pp.28-29.
3 "Tariff Authority for Major Ports", *Indian Infrastructure*, June 2004, p. 32.
4 Buddhadeb Ghosh and Prabir De (2001), "Indian Ports a Globalization Grounding Economics in Geography", *Economic and Political Weekly*, August 25, pp.3271-3283.
5 http://www.sarologistics.com/ports.html.
6 http://mospi.nic.in/Mospi_New/upload/Infra_stat_2010/3.ch_IWT.pdf.
7 http://en.wikipedia.org/wiki/Ports_in_India.
8 http://www.indiamaritimeindustryexpo.com/sector_inside.html.
9 http://www.performance.gov.in/sites/default/files/document/strategy/Shipping.pdf.

10 Maritime Agenda (2010-2020), Ministry of Shipping, Government of India, January, 2011.
11 Ibid.
12 Ibid.
13 Ibid.
14 http://www.ennoreport.gov.in/landlord.htm.
15 http://vizhinjamport.in/landlord.php.
16 http://www.indiacore.com/ports.html.
17 S. Sudalaimuthu, S. Anthony Raj, "Logistics Management for International Business: Text and Cases", Eastern Economy Edition, 2009.
18 http://www.kolkataporttrust.gov.in/land%20policy%202010.pdf.
19 Ibid.
20 http://www.thepriest.in/2011/07/modernization-of-indian-ports.html.
21 http://pib.nic.in/newsite/efeatures.aspx?relid=73382.
22 www.articlesbase.com/.../understanding-corporate-social-responsibility.
23 Maritime Agenda (2010-2020), Ministry of Shipping, Government of India, January, 2011.
24 Ibid.
25 Ibid.
26 Ibid.
27 Ibid.
28 Ibid.
29 Ibid.
30 Ibid.
31 Ibid.
32 Ibid.
33 Ibid.
34 http://www.articlesbase.com/business-articles/understanding-corporate-social-responsibility-2999225.html.
35 http://www.indiacsr.in/en/?p=2324.
36 Port Development, "A Handbook for Planners in Developing Countries", Second edition; Revised and Expanded, UNCTAD, United Nations, New York, 1985.
37 Ibid.
38 Maritime Agenda (2010-2020), Ministry of Shipping, Government of India, January, 2011.
39 Ibid.
40 Ibid.
41 http://www.performance.gov.in/sites/default/files/document/strategy/Shipping.pdf.
42 http://fcrm.ir/UserFiles/File/books/english/1604567120%20Globalization%20 Thrust.pdf.
43 http://www.indiawaterportal.org/sites/indiawaterportal.org/files/ Harbouring_trouble- The_social_and_environmental_upshot_of_port_ growth_ in_ India_ Dakshin_Foundation_2011.pdf.

44 Sudarshan Rodriguez and Aarthi Sridhar, "The Social and Environmental Upshot of Port Growth in India", Dakshin Foundation, 2010.

45 Christiaan Van Krimen LL.M., "Regulation of the Indian Port Sector", May 2011.

46 Ibid.

47 Ibid.

48 Position Paper on the Ports Sector in India, Department of Economic Affairs, Ministry of Finance, Government of India, December 2009.

APPENDICES

Appendix Table 1: Master Table for Computing Performance of Major Ports (2011–12)

Ports	*TRT (Days)*	*1/TRT*	*X-Mean/ S.D.*	*PBWT (Days)*	*1/TRT*	*X-Mean/ S.D.*	*NWTB (Days)*	*1/TRT*	*X-Mean/ S.D.*	*OSBD (Tonnes)*	*X-Mean/ S.D.*	*Cargo (MT)*	*X-Mean/ S.D.*	*No. of Vessels Sailed*	*X-Mean/ S.D.*
Kolkata	5.45	0.18	-0.78	0.77	1.30	1.49	1.16	0.86	-0.72	2503.00	-1.57	12.23	-1.45	1204.00	-0.44
Haldia	3.62	0.28	-0.12	2.54	0.39	-0.87	0.84	1.19	-0.58	6728.00	-0.90	31.01	-0.57	1962.00	0.51
Visakhapatnam	5.68	0.18	-0.83	2.84	0.35	-0.98	0.63	1.59	-0.40	10704.00	-0.26	67.42	1.14	2432.00	1.11
Chennai	3.91	0.26	-0.26	1.16	0.86	0.35	0.96	1.04	-0.64	10352.00	-0.32	55.71	0.59	2043.00	0.62
Tuticorin	4.94	0.20	-0.64	1.91	0.52	-0.53	0.77	1.30	-0.53	6733.00	-0.90	28.11	-0.70	1492.00	-0.08
Cochin	1.82	0.55	1.82	1.05	0.95	0.59	0.33	3.03	0.22	15784.00	0.54	20.09	-1.08	557.00	-1.26
New Mangalore	2.95	0.34	0.33	0.79	1.27	1.40	0.33	3.03	0.22	13957.00	0.25	32.94	-0.48	1136.00	-0.53
Mumbai	1.94	0.52	1.58	1.37	0.73	0.01	0.57	1.75	-0.33	6476.00	-0.94	56.18	0.62	1579.00	0.03
JNPT	2.46	0.41	0.81	1.13	0.88	0.41	0.29	3.45	0.40	19227.00	1.09	65.75	1.07	2892.00	1.69
Kandla	6.42	0.16	-0.98	3.74	0.27	-1.20	0.34	2.94	0.18	14272.00	0.30	82.50	1.85	2714.00	1.46
Paradip	6.33	0.16	-0.96	3.69	0.27	-1.19	0.62	1.61	-0.39	15995.00	0.58	54.25	0.52	1328.00	-0.29
Mormugao	7.68	0.13	-1.16	2.94	0.34	-1.01	0.95	1.05	-0.63	10530.00	-0.29	39.00	-0.19	500.00	-1.33
Ennore	2.17	0.46	1.19	0.76	1.32	1.53	0.10	10.00	3.22	27505.00	2.41	14.96	-1.32	385.00	-1.48

Source: Ministry of Shipping, Road Transport & Highways, Govt. of India.

Appendix Table 2: Master Table for Computing Performance of Major Ports (2008–09)

Ports	*TRT (Days)*	*1/TRT*	*X-Mean/ S.D.*	*PBWT (Days)*	*1/TRT*	*X-Mean/ S.D.*	*NWTB (Days)*	*1/TRT*	*X-Mean/ S.D.*	*OSBD (Tonnes)*	*X-Mean/ S.D.*	*Cargo (MT)*	*X-Mean/ S.D.*	*No. of Vessels Sailed*	*X-Mean/ S.D.*
Kolkata	4.60	0.22	-0.75	0.66	1.52	0.22	1.08	0.93	-0.63	3027.00	-1.30	12.43	-1.46	856.00	-0.46
Haldia	4.21	0.24	-0.57	3.38	0.30	-0.40	0.66	1.52	-0.40	7732.00	-0.57	41.79	0.05	1421.00	0.60
Visakhapatnam	3.93	0.25	-0.41	1.28	0.78	-0.15	0.53	1.89	-0.25	11171.00	-0.05	63.91	1.19	1571.00	0.89
Chennai	4.15	0.24	-0.54	1.39	0.72	-0.19	0.65	1.54	-0.39	10778.00	-0.11	57.49	0.86	1423.00	0.61
Tuticorin	3.66	0.27	-0.24	1.09	0.92	-0.08	0.72	1.39	-0.45	5817.00	-0.87	22.01	-0.97	935.00	-0.31
Cochin	2.14	0.47	1.52	0.70	1.43	0.18	0.48	2.08	-0.18	10599.00	-0.14	15.23	-1.32	831.00	-0.50
New Mangalore	3.00	0.33	0.30	0.65	1.54	0.24	0.37	2.70	0.07	13645.00	0.33	36.69	-0.21	803.00	-0.56
Mumbai	4.73	0.21	-0.81	1.41	0.71	-0.19	0.97	1.03	-0.59	5717.00	-0.88	51.88	0.57	1081.00	-0.03
JNPT	1.90	0.53	2.06	0.95	1.05	-0.01	0.09	11.11	3.38	20344.00	1.36	57.29	0.85	2061.00	1.81
Kandla	5.20	0.19	-0.98	2.62	0.38	-0.36	0.44	2.27	-0.10	13107.00	0.25	72.23	1.62	1859.00	1.43
Paradip	4.78	0.21	-0.83	2.32	0.43	-0.33	0.62	1.61	-0.36	12635.00	0.18	46.41	0.29	973.00	-0.24
Mormugao	3.61	0.28	-0.21	1.77	0.56	-0.27	0.55	1.82	-0.28	6290.00	-0.80	41.68	0.04	297.00	-1.51
Ennore	2.35	0.43	1.14	0.27	3.70	1.35	0.34	2.94	0.16	28424.00	2.60	11.50	-1.51	181.00	-1.73

Source: Ministry of Shipping, Road Transport & Highways, Govt. of India.

Appendix Table 3: Master Table for Computing Performance of Major Ports (2003–04)

Ports	*TRT (Days)*	*1/TRT*	*X-mean/ S.D.*	*PBWT (Days)*	*1/ PBWT*	*X-Mean/ S.D.*	*NWTB (Days)*	*1/ NWTB*	*X-Mean/ S.D.*	*OSBD (Tonnes)*	*X-Mean/ S.D.*	*Cargo in MT*	*X-Mean/ S.D.*	*No. of Vessels Sailed*	*X-Mean/ S.D.*
Kolkata	4.29	0.23	-0.88	0.51	1.98	-0.09	1.14	0.88	-1.30	3384.00	-1.05	8.69	-1.46	765.00	-0.79
Haldia	2.84	0.35	0.20	0.97	1.03	-0.35	0.73	1.37	-0.33	8280.00	-0.41	32.57	0.49	1889.00	0.52
Visakhapatnam	3.33	0.30	-0.27	0.76	1.32	-0.27	0.59	1.69	0.30	11712.00	0.04	47.74	1.73	1704.00	0.31
Chennai	4.85	0.21	-1.13	2.28	0.44	-0.51	1.03	0.97	-1.12	9517.00	-0.24	36.71	0.83	1656.00	0.25
Tuticorin	2.52	0.40	0.61	0.70	1.42	-0.24	0.76	1.32	-0.44	5084.00	-0.82	13.68	-1.05	1517.00	0.09
Cochin	2.22	0.45	1.10	0.43	2.30	0.00	0.59	1.69	0.30	7799.00	-0.47	13.57	-1.06	1133.00	-0.36
New Mangalore	2.35	0.43	0.87	0.55	1.82	-0.13	0.53	1.89	0.68	17955.00	0.86	26.67	0.01	879.00	-0.65
Mumbai	4.07	0.25	-0.77	0.87	1.15	-0.32	0.47	2.13	1.15	5911.00	-0.72	29.92	0.28	1800.00	0.42
JNPT	1.85	0.54	1.91	0.76	1.32	-0.27	1.23	0.81	-1.43	9845.00	-0.20	31.27	0.39	3681.00	2.61
Kandla	5.06	0.20	-1.20	2.03	0.49	-0.50	0.45	2.22	1.34	8659.00	-0.36	41.52	1.22	1823.00	0.44
Paradip	3.43	0.29	-0.35	0.53	1.89	-0.11	0.99	1.01	-1.04	10257.00	-0.15	25.31	-0.10	1041.00	-0.47
Mormugao	4.47	0.22	-0.97	2.60	0.38	-0.52	0.50	2.00	0.90	16746.00	0.70	27.87	0.11	677.00	-0.89
Ennore	2.11	0.47	1.31	0.07	14.29	3.28	0.49	2.04	0.98	32777.00	2.80	9.28	-1.41	166.00	-1.48

Source: Ministry of Shipping, Road Transport & Highways, Govt. of India.

Appendix Table 4: Master Table for Computing Performance of Major Ports (1996–97)

Ports	*TRT (Days)*	*1/TRT*	*X-Mean/ S.D.*	*PBWT (Days)*	*1/ PBWT*	*X-Mean/ S.D.*	*NWTB (Days)*	*1/ NWTB*	*X-Mean/ S.D.*	*OSBD (Tonnes)*	*X-Mean/ S.D.*	*Cargo in MT*	*X-Mean/ S.D.*	*No. of Vessels Sailed*	*X-Mean/ S.D.*
Kolkata	7.7	0.13	-0.80	0.95	1.05	1.90	2.66	0.38	-1.13	1188	-1.78	6.02	-1.15	874	-0.35
Haldia	6	0.17	-0.07	2.19	0.46	-0.31	1.55	0.65	-0.36	5855	0.30	17.1	-0.16	947	-0.24
Visakhapatnam	5.66	0.18	0.13	1.6	0.63	0.31	0.83	1.20	1.24	6696	0.68	34.5	1.39	1437	0.56
Chennai	7.8	0.13	-0.84	4.07	0.25	-1.09	1.82	0.55	-0.63	5131	-0.02	31.85	1.15	1681	0.95
Tuticorin	5.16	0.19	0.48	1.56	0.64	0.37	1.48	0.68	-0.27	3026	-0.96	9.18	-0.87	905	-0.30
Cochin	3.9	0.26	1.73	1.12	0.89	1.31	1.26	0.79	0.07	5438	0.12	11.74	-0.64	784	-0.50
New Mangalore	4.43	0.23	1.11	1.51	0.66	0.45	1.35	0.74	-0.08	7172	0.89	12.45	-0.58	644	-0.73
Mumbai	10.67	0.09	-1.53	4.57	0.22	-1.19	2.21	0.45	-0.91	2605	-1.15	33.73	1.32	2616	2.46
JNPT	6.3	0.16	-0.23	2.14	0.47	-0.27	0.71	1.41	1.82	2987	-0.98	8.07	-0.97	640	-0.73
Kandla	10.56	0.09	-1.51	6.61	0.15	-1.44	1.18	0.85	0.22	7066	0.84	33.73	1.32	1527	0.70
Paradip	4.9	0.20	0.68	1.61	0.62	0.30	0.8	1.25	1.37	6406	0.55	11.58	-0.66	557	-0.87
Mormugao	6.3	0.16	-0.23	2.2	0.45	-0.32	3.03	0.33	-1.26	8540	1.50	17.31	-0.15	507	-0.95

Source: Ministry of Shipping, Road Transport & Highways, Govt. of India.

Appendix Table 5: Master Table for Computing Performance of Major Ports (1991–92)

Ports	*TRT (Days)*	*1/TRT*	*X-Mean/ S.D.*	*PBWT (Days)*	*1/ PBWT*	*X-Mean/ S.D.*	*NWTB (Days)*	*1/ NWTB*	*X-Mean/ S.D.*	*OSBD (Tonnes)*	*X-Mean/ S.D.*	*Cargo in MT*	*X-Mean/ S.D.*	*No. of Vessels Sailed*	*X-Mean/ S.D.*
Kolkata	10.52	0.10	-1.62	0.75	1.33	1.70	3.44	0.29	-1.31	612.00	-1.55	4.00	-1.16	717.00	-0.25
Haldia	5.96	0.17	0.19	1.52	0.66	-0.41	1.62	0.62	0.41	5861.00	0.55	12.00	-0.18	703.00	-0.28
Visakhapatnam	5.58	0.18	0.48	1.02	0.98	0.59	1.23	0.81	1.44	6120.00	0.65	21.52	0.98	928.00	0.17
Chennai	5.98	0.17	0.18	1.56	0.64	-0.47	2.14	0.47	-0.38	4579.00	0.03	25.05	1.41	1381.00	1.09
Tuticorin	5.19	0.19	0.82	1.26	0.79	0.01	1.65	0.61	0.35	2196.00	-0.92	5.87	-0.93	724.00	-0.24
Cochin	3.95	0.25	2.33	0.79	1.27	1.49	1.44	0.69	0.81	4124.00	-0.15	7.48	-0.74	621.00	-0.44
New Mangalore	5.50	0.18	0.55	1.67	0.60	-0.60	1.83	0.55	0.03	4564.00	0.03	8.27	-0.64	452.00	-0.78
Mumbai	7.48	0.13	-0.66	1.55	0.65	-0.45	3.05	0.33	-1.12	2825.00	-0.67	26.26	1.56	2106.00	2.54
JNPT	8.59	0.12	-1.09	3.56	0.28	-1.59	1.61	0.62	0.43	5322.00	0.33	21.00	0.92	1022.00	0.36
Kandla	6.08	0.16	0.11	1.17	0.85	0.20	1.15	0.87	1.73	4919.00	0.17	7.30	-0.76	347.00	-1.00
Paradip	5.96	0.17	0.19	0.87	1.15	1.12	2.42	0.41	-0.67	10343.00	2.34	15.10	0.20	601.00	-0.48
Mormugao	10.52	0.10	-1.62	0.75	1.33	1.70	3.44	0.29	-1.31	612.00	-1.55	4.00	-1.16	717.00	-0.25

Source: Ministry of Shipping, Road Transport & Highways, Govt. of India.

Glossary

BERTH: A loading or discharging anchorage allowing a ship to go alongside.

BERTH-DAY: A day of occupation of a berth by a ship.

BERTH OCCUPANCY: The time in hours or in days spent at berth. The Berth occupancy rate is arrived at by dividing the time (in hours) spent by ships at berth by the total berth hours available during the month.

BUILD, OPERATE AND TRANSFER: Private operators build or rehabilitate facilities, which are eventually transferred to public ownership, also known as concessions.

CABOTAGE: Coastal trade; the movement of cargoes by ship between ports of the same coast or between ports of the same coast or between ports of the same country.

CELLULAR SHIP: A ship which is dedicated to the carriage of shipping containers.

COMBI: A combined ship. A ship specifically designed to carry both containers and conventional cargoes.

CONTAINER: Box; designed to enable goods to be sent from door to door without the contents being handled. The most common size of containers is the 20-footer which measures about 20 feet by 8 feet by 8 feet 6 inches.

CRANAGE: The hire charges for providing a port crane for cargo handling.

DRAUGHT (DRAFT): The depth necessary to submerge a ship to its load line.

ENTREPORT: A transit port where the imported goods can be stored for a time to be re-exported without paying any customs duty. Such stores are termed as transshipment cargo. Entreport is a French word, which literally means a warehouse or store.

FREIGHT: Charges quoted by the owners for the carriage of cargo.

FULL PRIVATISING: Implies that all assets and liabilities are transferred to the private sector.

IDLE TIME: Non-Working time of a ship (without loading or unloading of cargo) at berth.

JETTY: A light structure which can only support pipelines, conveyors and light vehicles.

JOINT VENTURES: Operators create a new independent company. This type of agreement arises when two or more parties with common interests join forces.

LEASING: The port authority leases port assets to private operators for a given period. In contrast to a concession, the private operators do not usually make investments and therefore only assume commercial risks.

LICENSING: Private operators provide services requiring basic equipments which they own. The port authority owns the port infrastructure and super-infrastructure and charges the private operators for their use.

MANAGEMENT CONTRACT: The port authority remains the owner of the port, but the port is run by a private firm, which provides for a more efficient management of operations.

OUTPUT PER BERTH DAY: The total tonnage handled distributed over the total number of berth days.

PILOTAGE: A port charge for guiding a ship in or out of a harbour through channels, passages or other waters by an authorised pilot.

PORT DUES: A levy of port authority on a ship.

PRE-BERTHING DETENTION: The time for which a ship waits before getting entry into a berth.

SHIP-DAY: A day spent in harbour by a ship.

SHIPYARD: The place where ships are built.

STEVEDORE: The person running a business, whose functions are to load, stow and unload ships; often used synonymously with docker.

TRAFFIC: A scalar with only magnitude but no direction such as the total of exports and imports or loaded and unloaded cargo.

TRAFFIC FLOW: A vector with magnitude and direction such as passengers embarked/disembarked or cargo exports/imports.

TURN-ROUND TIME: The total time spent by a ship since its entry till its departure.

WHARF: A structure built alongside the water where ships berth for loading or discharging goods.

WHARFARE: A port charge on the ships for all the cargo conveyed over or through a wharf/berth.

Bibliography

Books

Banga, Indu (ed.) (1992), *Port and Their Hinterlands in India 1700-1950*, Manohar Publication, New Delhi.

Batra, Satkartar (ed.) (1963), *Ports of Gujarat: West Coast of India*, Kandla Commercial, Kandla.

Chakravorty, A. (1995), *Status of Major Ports of India*, Indian Ports Association, New Delhi.

Institution of Civil Engineers (1991), *Ports into Next Century*, Thomas Telford, London.

Kamath, M. M. (1984), *Physical Planning of Ports and Various Types of Structures in Ports*, Indian Institute of Technology, Chennai.

Kindelberger, C.P. (1996), *World Economic Primacy: 1500-1990*, OPU, New York.

Monie, Gustaaf De (1991), *Port Modernization Study India*, World Bank, Washington.

Pearson, Michael N. (1998), *Port Cities and Intruders: the Swahili Coast, India and Portugal in the Early Modern Era*, The John Hopkins University Press, Baltimore.

Ray, A. (1993), *Maritime India: Ports and Shipping*, Pearl Publishers, Kolkata.

Sahai, Baldeo (1986), *The Ports of India*, Ministry of Information and Broadcasting Publication Division, Govt. of India, New Delhi.

Sridharan, K. Rear Admiral (1981), *A Maritime History of India*, Ministry of Information and Broadcasting, Publication Division, Govt. of India, New Delhi.

Taylor, G. Captain (1974), *Sea Ports: An Introduction to their Place and Purpose*, Glasgow Brown, Son and Ferguson Limited, Nautical Publishers, Great Britain.

Articles

Baird, Alfred J. (2001), "Trends in Port Privatisation", *Ports and Harbour*, Jan-Feb, pp.16-21.

Bandall, H.B. and Stent, A.F. (1987), "On Measuring Cargo Handling Productivity", *Maritime Policy and Management*, Vol. 14(4), pp. 56-67.

Batra, Satkartar (1988), "How Efficiency at Indian Ports can be Improved", *Indian Ports*, Jan-March, pp. 21-29.

Bauer, P.W. (1990), "Decomposing TFP Growth in the Presence of Cost Inefficiency, Nonconstant Returns to Scale, and Technological Progress", *Journal of Productivity Analysis*, Vol. 1(2), pp.105-16.

Bose, Santu Kumar (2001), "Cargo Handling of Major Ports in India: A Case Study", *Economic and Political Weekly*, August 25, pp.3284-3288.

Chakrabarty, S.N. (2000), "Analysis of Performance of Major Ports during the First Quarter of 1999-2000", *EXIM Shipping Times*, New Year Special Supplement, pp. 23-34.

Chakrabarty, S.N. and Das, Rebecca (2001), "Comparison of Performance of Major Ports of India during April to September 2000 through a Single Measure of Efficiency: Few Approaches", *Indian Ports*, Vol. 32(4), Apr., pp. 15-30.

Chandran, Harish (1991), "Cochin Port: The Performance Profile", *Indian Ports*, Vol. 31(1), July, pp. 49-51.

Christina, Beatty and Fothergill, Stephen (2004), "Economic Change and the Labour Market in Britain's Seaside Towns", *Regional Studies*, Vol. 38(5), July, pp. 461-480.

Clark, Ximena et al (2004), "Port Efficiency, Maritime Transport Costs, and Bilateral Trade", *Journal of Development Economics*, 75(2), Dec., pp. 417-50.

"Containerisation at Indian Ports attracts Major Global Players", *The Link Global Trade and Freight Review*, Vol. 10(5), May 2005, pp. 6-10.

De, P. (1999), "Performance of Indian Ports", *Indian Ports*, Vol. 31 (2), October, pp. 23-33.

De, P. and B. Chaudhury (1999), "Concentration of Indian Port System: 1970-1998", *Foreign Trade Review*, Vol. 35(1), Oct.-Dec., pp. 128-56.

De, P. and Ghosh (2001), "Technological Change, Productivity and Performance: A Case Study of Indian Ports under Globalisation", paper presented at *The 9th World Conferences on Transport Research*, held at Seoul, Korea during July 22-27.

De, Prabir (1999), "Performance of Indian Ports", *Journal of Indian Ports*, Vol. 31(2), October, pp 5-10.

De. Prabir and T.K. Palit (2001), "Impact of Performance on Traffic: Evidence from Major Ports of India", *Indian Ports*, Vol. 32(3), Jan., pp.27-35.

Department of Industrial Policy and Promotion (2014), Annual Report 2014 15 "Make in India", Ministry of Commerce and Industry, Government of India.

Dion, Stephane et al (2002), "Port and Airport Divestiture in Canada: A Comparative Analysis", *Journal of Transport Geography*, Sept., 10(30), pp.187-193.

Fujita, M and Mori (2000), "Structural Stability and Evolution of Urban System", *Regional Science and Urban Economics*, Vol. 34(8), pp. 45-56.

Ghosh, Buddhadeb and De, Prabir (2001), "Indian Ports a Globalization Grounding Economics in Geography", *Economic and Political Weekly*, August 25, pp.3271-3283.

"Guidelines for Private Sector Participation in Ports through Joint Ventures and Foreign Collaboration Issued by the Central Government", *Indian Ports*, Vol. 30(1), July 1998, pp. 15-18.

Hershman, Mare J. and Chamberlin, Katie M. (2003), "Port – City Change and Growth: Examples from the Pacific Northwest of the U.S.", *Korea Observer*, 34(3), Autumn, pp. 485-507.

Iyer, K.V.A. (2003), "Port Sector Reforms: Global Compulsions and Domestic Concerns", *Indian Port*, Vol. 35(1), pp.17-18.

Iyer, K.V.A. (2004), "Refining Seaport Privatisation – Indian Experience", *Indian Ports*, Jan., pp. 19-23.

Kidwai, Atiya and Kuzur, Gloria, "Seaports, Dry Ports and Development Corridors: Implications for Regional Development in Globalizing India", Working Paper 178, February 2015, Institute for Studies in Industrial Development, New Delhi.

Kotak, Krishna (2001), "Privatisation of Ports", *Times Shipping Journal*, Vol. 1(8), p. 36.

Kumar, R. Sasi and Bhasi, M. (2003), "Operational Problems of Modern Container Terminals", *Indian Port*, Vol. 35(4), Oct., pp. 5-10.

Kumar, R. Sasi and Bhasi, M. (2004), "A Comparative Study of Performance of India's Major Sea Ports", *Indian Ports*, Vol. 36(2), Oct., pp. 9-18.

"Maritime Agenda (2010-2020)", Ministry of Shipping, Government of India, January, 2011.

McCalla, Robert J. (1999), "Global Change and Local Pain: Intermodal Seaport Terminals and Their Service Areas", *Journal of Transport Geography*, 7(4), Dec., pp. 247-54.

Ministry of Micro, Small and Medium Enterprises (2013), *Recommendations of the Inter Ministerial Committee for Accelerating Manufacturing in Micro, Small and Medium Enterprises Sector*, New Delhi: Government of India, September.

Misro, R.C. and Panigrani, N.P. (1999), "Ports of South Orissa during the Ninteenth Century AD: A Historical Reappraisal", *Journal of Indian Ocean studies*, Vol. 7(10), Nov., pp. 38-47.

Mukherjee, S. (2001), "A Time to Change", *Indian Ports*, Vol. 32(3), Jan., pp. 17-21.

Noronha, Ernesto (2003), "Globalisation: The Impact on Port and Dock Workers in India", *Indian Journal of Labour Economics*, 46(4), (Oct.-Dec.), pp. 611-21.

"Port Services: A Fragmented Industry Dominated by a Handful of Operators", *Indian Infrastructure*, July 2001.

"Private Participation in Ports: Picking Up at Last", *Indian Infrastructure*, July 2001, pp. 24.

Quasim, S.Z. (2002), "Degradation of Indian Estuaries and Measures for Their Protection", *Journal of Indian Ocean Studies*, Vol. 10(1), Apr., pp. 100-08.

Ramakrishanan, R. (2003), "Scenario of Port Handling and Vision", *Indian Ports,* Vol. 35(2), Oct., pp. 5-17.

Ramakrishnan, R. (2002), "Indian Ports' Performance", *The Link*, Feb., pp. 26-29.

Raman, M. (2004), "Corporatisation of Ports: It is the Way Forward?" *Indian Ports*, Vol. 35(3), Jan., pp. 5-6.

Ranade, Prabha Shastri (2001),"Impact of Infrastructure Development on the Ports of India's Western Coast", *Foreign Trade Review*, pp. 69-84.

Rodriguez, Sudarshan and Sridhar, Aarthi (2010), "Harbouring Trouble: The Social and Environmental Upshot of Port Growth in India", *Dakshin Foundation.*

Rosa, Luigi de (2002), "Naples: A Maritime Port", *Journal of European Economic History*, Winter, Vol. 31(3), pp. 513-30.

Sudalaimuthu S. and Raj, S. Anthony (2009), "Logistics Management for International Business: Text and Cases", Eastern Economy Edition.

Sarkar, J. (2002), "Corporatisation of Major Ports", *Indian Port*, Vol. 33(3), July, pp.31-36.

Sarkar, J. (2002), "Principle of Traffic Forecasting", *Indian Ports*, July, pp. 9-12.

Sinha, Shatrughan (in an interview) (2003), "Ports of Future", *Geography and You*, 3(9), Sep., pp. 31-32.

Song, Dong and Wook (2002), "Regional Container Port Competition and Cooperation: The Case of Hong Kong and South China", *Journal of Transport Geography*, June, Vol. 10(2), pp. 99-100.

Srinivas, K.T. (2013), "Role of Micro, Small and Medium Enterprises in Inclusive Growth", *International Journal of Engineering and Management Research*, Vol. 3(4), pp. 57-61.

Subrahmanyam, Sanjay (2000), "Note on the Rise of Surat in the Sixteenth Century", *Journal of the Economic and Social History of the Orient*, Vol. 43(1), Feb., pp. 23-33.

The Sagarmala Project, *Indian Infrastructure*, Vol. 6(7), Feb. 2004.

Turnbull, Peter and Wass, Victoria (1995), "Great Dock and Dole Swindle: Accounting for the Costs and Benefits of Ports Transport Deregulation and the Dock Labour Compensation Scheme", *Public Administration*, Winter, Vol. 73(40), pp. 513-34.

UNCTAD Report (1976), "Port Performance Indicators", United Nations Conference on Trade and Development, United Nations, Geneva, New York.

Newspapers

"An Agenda for Indian Maritime Industry", *Economic Times*, dated 2nd Dec. 2004.

"Improvement in Ports' Throughput", *Businessline*, dated 10th May 2005.

"Port Guidelines", *Business Standard*, dated 5th May 2005.

"Special Features on Indian Ports", *Business Roundup*, dated 25th June 2004.

"What the Major Ports Moved and How Much", *Businessline*, dated 2nd May 2005.

Government Reports and Documents

"Major Ports-Performance Round-up", *Indian Infrastructure*, June 2002, pp. 28-30.

"Port Financing: Still A Trickle", *Indian Infrastructure*, July 2001, pp. 28-29.

"Port Policy and Privatisation", *Indian Infrastructure*, Vol. 4(4), June 2002, pp. 24-25.

"Port Policy: Opening up the Sector in Phases", *Indian Infrastructure*, July 2001, p. 23.

"Port Sector: Coping with Growth", *Indian Infrastructure*, July 2001, p. 22.

"Report of the Major Port Reforms Commission", Ministry of Shipping and Transport, Government of India, New Delhi, 1968.

"Report on Major Ports", Ministry of Shipping and Transport, Government of India, New Delhi, 1970.

Economic Survey, Government of India, Ministry of Finance, Economic Division, 2004-05.

Government of India, Ministry of Surface Transport (1999), "Analysis of Relative Physical Performance of Major Ports during 1998-99".

India Year Book compiled and edited by the Research, Reference and Training Division, Publication Division, Ministry of Information and Broadcasting Government of India, 2004 and 2005.

Perspective Plan for Indian Port Sector Vision 2020, Ministry of Shipping Govt. of India Volume II, Apr 2001, Rites Ltd.(A Govt. of India Enterprise), New Delhi.

UNCTAD (1976), "Port Performance Indicators", New York.

Unpublished Documents

Gupta, Sadanand, "Restructuring of Major Ports in India in the Post Reform Era (1991-2004)" MPhil Dissertation, Unpublished, 2005, CSRD/SSS/JNU, New Delhi.

Sarkar, Kakali (2000), "The Port System in India; An Analysis of the Hierarchical Changes and Port Performance (1950-1995)", Unpublished PhD Thesis, CSRD/SSS/JNU, New Delhi.

Referred Internet Sites

Container Corporation of India, http://www.concorindia.com

Deloitte (2012), "National Conference on Container Infrastructure in India", Background Paper 3. Available at: http://3six5ive.net/dogfen/national conference on container infrastructure inindia 188833/

http://en.wikipedia.org/wiki/Ports_in_India.

http://mospi.nic.in/Mospi_New/upload/Infra_stat_2010/3.ch_IWT.pdf.

http://pib.nic.in/newsite/efeatures.aspx?relid=73382.

http://vizhinjamport.in/landlord.php.

http://www.ennoreport.gov.in/landlord.htm.

http://www.indiacore.com/ports.html.

http://www.indiamaritimeindustryexpo.com/sector_inside.html.

http://www.indiawaterportal.org/sites/indiawaterportal.org/files/Harbouring_trouble- The_social_and_environmental_upshot_of_port_ growth_ in_ India_ Dakshin_Foundation_2011.pdf.

http://www.ipa.nic.in/

http://www.kolkataporttrust.gov.in/land%20policy%202010.pdf.

http://www.oecd.org/countries/mongolia/42228028.pdf

http://www.performance.gov.in/sites/default/files/document/strategy/Shipping.pdf.

http://www.sagarsandesh.com/news/containerization-challenges.

http://www.sarologistics.com/ports.html.

http://www.thepriest.in/2011/07/modernization-of-indian-ports.html.

http://www.unmillenniumproject.org/documents/MainReportComplete-lowres.pdf

L. Lakshmanan, "Public-Private Partnership in Indian Infrastructure Development: Issues and Options", http://www.rbi.org.in/scripts/BS_VIEWContent.aspx?ID=1912.

National Conference on Container Infrastructure in India 2012, Background Paper. (http://www.deloitte.com/assets/DcomIndia/Local%20Assets/Documents/Thoughtware/Containerization%20Infrastructure%20 in%20India%201402_Final.pdf)

www.csi-vizag.org/LinkClick.aspx?

Index